Traitors Beware

Traitors Beware

A History of Robert DePugh's Minutemen

Eric Beckemeier

First Edition
Published by Eric Beckemeier
Hardin, MO

ISBN: 978-0-6151-7283-5

Library of Congress Control Number: 2007908436

To
Dr. Dane Miller, my mentor, for all his support and
assistance with this project

and to
Bob DePugh. Without his cooperation this book
would not have been possible

Contents

Author's Note

The idea for publishing a book concerning Robert DePugh's Minutemen first came to me while I was a freshman at the University of Central Missouri, formerly known as Central Missouri State University, studying for a degree in Criminal Justice. I was a member of the Honors College at the university and one of the requirements for graduation was the completion of a lengthy project. Although there were many different routes to take towards completion of the project, I knew that I would most likely end up writing a research paper, somewhat like an undergraduate thesis. The only thing left to do was decide on a topic.

I grappled with different ideas for an Honors Project topic. The idea of writing my paper about the Minutemen was always in the back of my mind but I often dismissed the idea for two reasons. First, the Minutemen were not a traditional topic for a Criminal Justice paper. Although I was not required to pick a topic that fit closely into my major, I thought that I should stick to my expertise. At that time extremist groups fell well out of my area of expertise. Second, I felt there was a danger of being considered an extremist myself by my professors and peers if I took such a great interest in an extremist organization. However, as I did more research concerning the Minutemen both of my reservations about writing my Honors Project concerning the group proved unfounded. I found that the Minutemen would be a very fitting topic for a Criminal Justice major because one cannot study the Minutemen without also studying law enforcement and the justice system of the 1960s. Secondly, I decided that the Minutemen was such an interesting topic that few could deny having at least a passing interest in the group. In that case I doubted that I would be considered an extremist for doing my Honors Project on the Minutemen. Also, by that point in my college career I did not really care whether or not I was considered an extremist by my peers and professors. Whatever the case, I do not think that my choice of a topic has adversely affected my reputation at the university. My final decision to write about the Minutemen may have also been affected by that fact that I could not think of any other topic I was more interested in writing about at the time than the Minutemen.

Robert DePugh's Minutemen had always fascinated me. This may seem surprising to the reader because the Minutemen were disbanded before I was even born. However, I grew up around Norborne, Missouri, where Robert DePugh lived for much of the existence of the Minutemen and where many of the organization's activities took place. I grew up hearing stories about the Minutemen from my peers and even from my schoolteachers on occasion. Like much of the information commonly found concerning the Minutemen, these stories were often more fiction than fact. As is often the case it was the fiction that first caught my interest.

The Minutemen had attained almost a mythical status in Norborne, Missouri by the time I was in elementary school. Stories were often told about caches of weapons and explosives belonging to the Minutemen being found in the town some years earlier. Although based somewhat on fact these stories were greatly exaggerated. One even boasted that there had been enough explosives in one building to blow up the whole town. Tales of tunnels under the town that had been dug by the Minutemen abounded. Some people even claimed to have found these tunnels and that they themselves had been in them. However, research for this book has found no evidence of any tunnels. The closest thing to a tunnel may have been a half-dug bomb shelter in the basement of one of DePugh's buildings. Stories about undercover FBI agents conducting surveillance on the DePugh house were also common. Of all of the stories, the ones concerning government surveillance were probably the most factual.

Under these conditions of abundant storytelling, I grew up with quite an interest in the Minutemen. When I finally got to college and had access to a large library I decided to do my first research concerning the organization. What I found was a lack of information concerning the Minutemen even in the library of a mid-sized university. However, this did not deter me and I continued researching and found many resources on the internet. Many of them were long out of print books that I was able to purchase used. In this way I learned about the Minutemen and after deciding to write my Honors Project about them, it became obvious to me that my earlier idea of writing a book about the Minutemen had finally become a real possibility. So in the course of events I first wrote *Traitors Beware* for my Honors Project at the University of Central Missouri. After receiving several requests from friends and family who were interested in reading the project, I determined that the time had finally come to publish it in book form. The result is this first paperback edition of *Traitors Beware*.

At this point I should note that I have retained almost entirely the original format of the Honors Project for this book. While the reader may not be familiar with the format, I found two very compelling reasons for retaining the original American Psychological Association (APA) format. First, since I am publishing this book without any assistance from editors I thought it would be wise to use a format that I was very familiar with. In this manner errors in citations and otherwise should be limited. Second, I think the APA format allows the reader to easily check out the sources I have used. There is much information concerning the Minutemen that is incorrect. It is an almost impossible task to completely separate fact from fiction concerning the Minutemen. As a result, there may be information in this book that is incorrect. However, the APA format allows the reader to easily find my sources of information. In that manner the reader who believes they have found incorrect information in this book can more easily find where that information originated. On that note I welcome anyone who believes they have found incorrect information to contact me so that future editions of this work can be as factual as possible.

Finally, the appendix to this book contains the entire transcript of a tape recorded interview with Robert De-Pugh. I do not pretend to be an expert in transcribing tape recordings into print. As a result, the transcript may not be easy to read but I assure the reader that it is very accurate. I included the interview transcript partially because I refer to it often throughout the book. It also contains so much information from DePugh that is not readily available other places that I thought deemed it necessary to include the entire transcript in this book. While I understand that readers often skip the appendix when reading a book, I believe that this interview transcript will be very interesting to the reader. It gives the reader a sense of how DePugh feels about the Minutemen years after the organization's downfall as well as providing much interesting information.

I hope that the reader will approach this book with an open mind about the Minutemen. Also, I hope the reader will consider the time in which the Minutemen briefly flourished when reading this book. Finally, I hope the reader enjoys this book and finds the answers to any nagging questions they may have concerning Bob DePugh's Minutemen.

Preface

The Minutemen, under Robert DePugh's leadership, existed for a relatively short period of years during the 1960s. They were a viciously anti-Communist organization that believed a Communist invasion of the United States was imminent, most likely through internal subversion. The organization advocated extremist tactics in what they believed was going to be a guerilla war against communism on American soil. Eventually the Minutemen's extreme nature and propensity for violence brought them to the attention from law enforcement. After Robert DePugh and other members were convicted of firearms violations and sent to prison, the leaderless organization faded into obscurity. The problem is previous research on the Minutemen is lacking and what research has been done is often severely biased against the organization. The purpose of this work is to provide an accurate historical record of the Minutemen.

The Minutemen organization has by now faded from the memories of most, especially of the younger generations who were not yet alive during the time of the Minutemen. Only one book has been written prior to this work that devotes all of its pages to the Minutemen. That book is even out of print at the time of this writing. In fact, very little mention is made of the Minutemen in contemporary books concerning extremist and radical groups. The Minutemen have in fact faded into obscurity as so many wished they would do during the 1960s. However, with that fade into obscurity the Minutemen have also been largely forgotten. At the current rate very few people will have heard of the Minutemen in thirty of forty years. It is for this reason that this book is being published. It is not being published to remember the Minutemen as a kind of memorial. It is being published to remember the Minutemen as a piece of history. History is always worth remembering. No matter how small or insignificant the group or event might have been. History is worth remembering because of the very real possibility that it might provide beneficial information at some unknown point in the future.

There is also a vast amount of information concerning the Minutemen that is not entirely based on fact. For this reason it is necessary to sort through the fact and the fiction concerning the Minutemen and separate the two as best as is possible. The fact must be separated and preserved because if interspersed with fiction the combination of the two adds little of value to the historical record. As the years pass it becomes increasingly difficult to separate the fact and the fiction. This work would not have been possible without Robert DePugh who is aging and in increasingly poor health as these words are written. As those with the memories die, the memories die also. The truth concerning the Minutemen is valuable and hopefully this book will help to spread the truth into the minds of the people.

Traitors Beware

Chapter One

An Introduction to the Minutemen

The term minuteman probably conjures up images of Paul Revere and the early American revolutionaries in the minds of most. However, the 1960s saw an entirely different type of revolutionary minutemen. These were Robert DePugh's Minutemen. The following pages will discuss these Minutemen of the 1960s in depth. The purpose of this book is to provide an accurate historical record of the Minutemen organization. The problem is that previous research is lacking and what research has been done is often severely biased against the organization.

Some explanation of what the Minutemen organization was is in order first. According to Evelyn A. Schlatter (2003), the Minutemen were "an organization dedicated to armed resistance against a Communist takeover of the United States" (p. 38). Daniel Levitas (2002) quoted a Federal Bureau of Investigation (FBI) report from 1965 saying the Minutemen were "a tiny, paramilitary group of rabidly anti-communist vigilantes" (p.72). Harry and Overstreet (1964) describe the Minutemen as follows: "A group…which trains itself in the tactics of guerilla warfare against the time of a Communist invasion" (p. 218). Isserman and Kazin (2000) note that the Minutemen were a violent organization (p. 212). The Minutemen were essentially a loosely organized band of guerrilla fighters who planned to defend the United States against what they considered to be an imminent Communist invasion. The Minutemen seemed to have considered the most probable route the Communist invasion would take would be through political and psychological conquest of the United States government and not through a military conflict (DePugh, 1970, p. 23). The Minutemen may have organized because of their belief that the United States government was incapable or unwilling to defend itself against such an attack. Whatever the reason the Minutemen formed, there is no doubt that they strongly opposed communism. As a result of the Minutemen's extremely anti-Communist attitude they have generally been considered an ultra-conservative or right wing group. However, there is a problem with applying such a simple label to a wide variety of organizations that include the John Birch Society, the Ku Klux Klan, the National States Rights Party, and others. Phillip Finch (1983) quoted DePugh's own explanation of the problem of applying labels:

> Radical right doesn't mean much. You could call it the American nationalist movement, but not everybody who's part of it is really a nationalist. A lot of people call it the patriotic movement, but you're being generous to call some of these people patriots. This brings us back to 'radical right,' and maybe that's as good a term as any, if you're going to use one. (p. 8)

Despite this problem with applying labels, Robert DePugh and his Minutemen have been called militants, radicals, racists, supremacists, kooks, nuts, and a variety of other names. This work should clarify what the Minutemen were and what they were not. However, there is no doubt that Robert DePugh and his followers were exceptionally controversial and extreme even during a time of great controversy and extremism.

There are several important topics that merit discussion in order to provide the most accurate record of the Minutemen that is possible. A biography of Robert DePugh is necessary because DePugh founded the Minutemen and was their only known leader. A discussion of how the Minutemen formed is essential to understanding how a group such as the Minutemen could ever have come into existence. Also, a discussion of the purpose of the Minutemen is necessary in order to clarify a variety of common misconceptions about this organization. Understanding the structure of the organization is necessary to understand the size and scope of the Minutemen and why the organization eventually fell apart. It is also important to understand the controversial nature of the Minutemen in order to explain their many conflicts with the government and other organizations. The federal government's crackdown on the Minutemen is also necessary to discuss because it highlights the organization's many controversial and sometimes illegal activities. Finally, it is necessary to discuss the effects of the Minutemen on the radical right, on communism, on politics and government, on society, and on those involved with the organization. After a discussion of all of these topics the reader should have a complete and accurate understanding of what the Minutemen organization was and what it was not.

Before the Minutemen can be discussed any further it is necessary to have some understanding of the time in which they briefly flourished. According to Farber and Roche (2003), the 1960's were a time of liberalism. It was a time of protest, rebellion, and social change. Civil rights and anti-war protests were the norm. Drug use was common. The Cold War was at its climax and there was a legitimate fear of a hot war that might include nuclear weapons. There was the war in Vietnam and the assassinations of President John F. Kennedy, Robert Kennedy, and Martin Luther King, Jr. Overall it was a time during which many questioned authority. However, conservatism never died. Even during the heyday of liberalism there was still a general consensus of anti-communism among the American people (p. 1). However, some conservatives also dared to question authority. As this paper will describe, the Minutemen were among those that questioned authority.

It is also necessary to have some basic understanding of communism since the Minutemen's primary enemy seemed to be the perceived Communist threat. According to Microsoft Encarta Encyclopedia (2002), communism strives to create social and economic equality among all people. Under communism, property is owned by the community or government. Each person is supposed to receive an equal share of the wealth and to do an equal share of the work. Communism is supposed to end the exploitation of the working class. A true Communist society would be classless. Karl Marx and Friedrich Engels created the modern theory of communism (para. 2). However, communism has never worked well in practice. Oppressive governments have tended to result, and the poor have generally remained poor. Communist governments have yet to create a classless society in which all people are equally prosperous. According to Microsoft Encarta Encyclopedia (2002), "as a result of Lenin's and Stalin's policies, many people came to associate the term communism with undemocratic or totalitarian governments that claimed allegiance to Marxist-Leninist ideals" (para. 3).

It is also important to understand DePugh's own views on communism to understand why he opposed it. According to DePugh (n.d.), communism is a utopian theory which has never and cannot be achieved. He also believed that communism does not account for differences in individuals and thus cannot succeed in practice (p. 4). "Some people are naturally hard working and ambitious while others are lazy. Some people are thrifty while others are wasteful" (DePugh, n.d., p. 4). DePugh (n.d.) believed that communism was a social system (p.1). It was a social system which he opposed to such an extent that he formed a paramilitary organization to defend the United States from it. DePugh (n.d) stated that the alternative to communism was individualism and that individualism meant freedom (p. 9). He goes on to state: "There is only one way to fight communism. We must take up the battle for individualism" (p 10). From DePugh's statements about communism it is not too difficult to understand his philosophy about it and why he believed individualism was the only solution. It seems that DePugh hated communism so passionately and perceived it as being so threatening to the freedom of all Americans that he was willing to take many risks in order to fight it.

Before further examining the Minutemen it is necessary to point out the paucity of existing research concerning the organization. By far the best source of information about the Minutemen is the work of J. Harry Jones, Junior. In fact, he has published the only book that examines the Minutemen in depth. Other publications concerning conservatism and right wing extremists groups also provide some useful information. Newspaper articles from the time are somewhat useful but are often biased and sometimes contain information that may not be entirely based on fact. In fact, Robert DePugh himself may be one of the better sources of information concerning the

Minutemen and he will be quoted and paraphrased often in the pages to come.

The methods used in research for this work included in depth searches of online bookstores for literature concerning the Minutemen. Most books and other literature concerning the Minutemen are long out of print and must be obtained used through online booksellers. Libraries are not generally good sources for information concerning the Minutemen because they tend to have information concerning conservative movements but not the Minutemen specifically. Also, much of the information concerning the Minutemen can only be obtained through Minutemen publications which rarely found their way into university libraries.

Searches of newspaper and periodical archives provide much information concerning the Minutemen. They are useful because they provide a view of the Minutemen during the time of their existence. However, the researcher must be wary of their accuracy and commonly biased nature.

A personal interview with Robert DePugh is a very useful research tool. DePugh is the only source of some information concerning the Minutemen and he is useful in filling in the gaps left by other sources. DePugh's reliability as a source of information concerning the Minutemen has been questioned in the past, and perhaps for good reason. However, since the Minutemen are no longer organized, DePugh has very little reason to provide deceptive information today.

Chapter Two

Robert DePugh before the Minutemen

According to Jones (1968), Robert 'Bob' Bolivar DePugh was born in April, 1923, in Independence, Missouri. He went by his middle name through adolescence. He was given his middle name by his father who named him after the South American revolutionary Simón Bolívar, who led revolts against Spanish rule in several South American countries (p. 23). Ralph DePugh was Bolivar's father. Ralph DePugh was a sheriff's deputy for Jackson County, Missouri during Bolivar's childhood. Ralph was closely connected to the Pendergast political machine, whose leader was the well known Tom Pendergast (pp. 22-23). According to Jones (1968), the elder DePugh "was …. a precinct captain for the dominant Democratic machine" (p. 23). Bolivar DePugh himself credits growing up around political corruption with giving him "a pretty cynical attitude toward the democratic process" (p. 23). He seemed to believe that most voters were more influenced by the media and the political machines than the quality of the candidates. Not much more is known of DePugh until he was in high school.

DePugh attended William Chrisman high school in Independence, Missouri where he was active in the Junior Reserve Officer Training Corps (JROTC). He was also secretary of the Wildlife Conservation Club and a member of the Radio Club. He graduated in 1941 in a class of 261 students (Jones, 1968, p. 23). During high school Bolivar DePugh attained grades that were average or slightly above average. However, he was very interested in physics and excelled in the subject (p. 23-24). DePugh explained his personality during high school in an interview with Jones (1968):

> I was pretty much an introvert. I didn't mix too well. It seemed a lot more people knew me than I knew them. I wasn't popular. I didn't have a great many friends. I was interested in amateur radio and had my own license and my own station and I spent most of my time working on my different pieces of electronic equipment and chatting with other ham operators around over the world.... (p. 24)

Alex Pertrovic, a classmate of DePugh's, confirmed De-Pugh's description of himself but added the Bolivar was difficult to talk to and that his classmates never took him seriously (Jones, 1968, p. 24).

According to Jones (1968), Bolivar DePugh developed his distaste for communism from his maternal grandmother who he says was quite politically aware. De-Pugh explained that she thought that the United States should stay out of World War II and let the Communists and Fascists fight each other to a point of what she believed would be mutual destruction (p. 25). DePugh also opposed the United States' involvement in the war in Europe. When asked by Jones (1968) in the mid-1960s if he still believed the United States made a mistake in entering World War II he believed that it did (p. 25).

Bolivar DePugh also read some books while he was in high school that might be considered unusual books for a young man to read. DePugh told Jones (1968) that he read Hitler's *Mein Kampf* three times. He also read *Das Kapital, The Communist Manifesto,* and *The Collected Works of Lenin* (p. 25-26).

According to Jones (1968), Bolivar DePugh attended the University of Missouri-Columbia in the fall of 1941 after graduating high school. He proclaimed his academic interest to be electrical engineering (p. 26). In an interview with DePugh (October 20, 2006), DePugh stated that he attended the University of Missouri for a year and a half (See Appendix). According to Jones (1968), DePugh joined the army in 1942. After joining the army DePugh was sent to Colorado. It is at this point that he claims to have studied radar as a civilian at the University of Colorado (p. 26). During an interview with DePugh (October 20, 2006), he said that he studied at the University of Colorado for a year during this time but did not specify his area of study (See Appendix). According to Schlatter (2003), the University of Colorado has no record of DePugh ever attending the school (p. 41). Schlatter (2003) cites an article from the *New York Times* titled "Minutemen's Soft–Sell Leader: Robert B. DePugh" (1961), which confirms "The University of Colorado has no record of Mr. DePugh's attending or of its ever having offered a radar training course" (p76).

In addition to the question of whether or not DePugh ever attended the University of Colorado, there is also speculation about the dates he served in the United States military. Schlatter (2003) reports that the only record the Department of Defense has for Robert DePugh is that he served in the Coast Artillery in Fort Monroe, Virginia from 1943 to 1944 (p. 41). Again she cites the same *New York Times* article mentioned earlier. However, this conflicts with Jones (1968) who maintains that DePugh enlisted in the army in 1942 (p. 26). Despite this contradiction and the question of whether or not he ever attended the University of Colorado, it is almost certain that DePugh was in Colorado between 1942 and 1943 because he met and married his wife while he was there (Jones, 1968, p. 27).

Jones (1968) goes on to note that DePugh served at Fort Monroe, Virginia between 1943 and the summer 1944 working with radar-jamming equipment (p. 27). DePugh was discharged from the army on August 31, 1944 after attaining the rank of private first class for a reason that was not publicly known until many years later. In 1966, while attempting to discover whether or not DePugh was mentally competent to stand trial, the prosecution exposed that he had been discharged for psychological reasons (p. 27-28). Jones (1968) quoted the army's report which stated that DePugh suffered from the following:

> Psychoneurosis, mixed type, severe, manifested by anxiety and depressive features and schizoid personality. Soldier is unable to perform duty due to anxiety, nervousness and mental depression. This condition is chronic and for three years has been attended with vague auditory hallucinations and mild ideas of reference. (p. 27)

Jones (1968) included DePugh's own thoughts about his discharge. DePugh claimed he was only sick at the time of his interview with the psychiatrist and that he thought the reason for his discharge was that the war was practically over. He claimed the psychiatrist who interviewed him was very busy at the time of the interview and did not spend a substantial amount of time conducting the interview. DePugh also claimed he did not take the interview seriously (p. 28-29). Jones (1968) quoted DePugh concerning the psychiatric interview: "I knew I was getting out. I didn't give a damn what he put down there. That was the way I thought about it at the time. I hardly remember it. And of course, I never knew anything about it" (p. 29). Despite evidence of mental illness while in the army, DePugh was found competent, by Judge Elmo B. Hunter, to stand trial in the 1966 case (George & Wilcox, 1996, p. 235).

According to Jones (1968), DePugh enrolled at Kansas State University in January of 1946 where he attended for a year and a half but did not complete a degree program (p. 29). In an interview with DePugh (October 20, 2006), he confirms that he did attend Kansas State University but for two and a half years instead of a year and a half (See Appendix). It is possible that this discrepancy in numbers resulted because DePugh may have attended Kansas State again after Jones' publication was completed. However, Schlatter (2003) claims that there is no record of DePugh ever attending Kansas State University either (p. 41). Schlatter (2003) also cites Jones (1968) and must be incorrect. Jones (1968) notes that while at Kansas State University DePugh "founded something called the Society for the Advancement of Canine Genetics which came to publish a periodical titled *The Journal of Canine Genetics*" (p. 29).

In an interview with DePugh (October 20, 2006), when questioned about his level of educational attainment, he replied that he had no college degrees. In addition to attending the University of Missouri, the University of Colorado, and Kansas State University, DePugh also says he attended Washburn University for a semester as well as taking some correspondence courses from Georgia Tech. His area of concentration was biochemistry in most of his higher educational pursuits (See Appendix). The *New York*

Times article titled "Minutemen's Soft-Sell Leader: Robert B. DePugh" confirms that "he took courses at the University of Missouri, Kansas State University, and Washburn University in Topeka" (p. 76). In matters where DePugh's records of attendance at various schools are concerned it would seem the DePugh would have very little reason to deceive the researcher so many years after the downfall of the Minutemen. His recent statements should probably be given preference when attempting to determine fact.

According to Schlatter (2003), DePugh became a salesman around 1947 and worked for several different companies selling various products. Schlatter (2003) also claims that in 1953 Robert and his wife, Ramona Van DePugh, moved back to Missouri (p. 41). However, there is reason to believe that DePugh was back in Independence in 1952. Jones (1968) tells us that DePugh made an unsuccessful attempt at running for public office in Missouri during 1952. He ran for the U.S. House of Representatives for Missouri's Fourth Congressional District in the Democratic primary in 1952 but never planned on winning. It was the same year his father ran unsuccessfully for sheriff in Jackson County (p. 29). Jones (1968) says that according to both Robert and Ralph DePugh, Robert planned on withdrawing from the race in time to keep his name off the ballot but missed the deadline (p. 29). Jones (1968) goes on to tell us that DePugh only filed to run in the primary "as part of a time-honored, faction endorsement-swapping tradition in Jackson County Democratic politics (p.29). Whatever the case, DePugh received only one thousand seven hundred seventy-four votes compared to the winner's thirty thousand (p. 29).

Jones (1968) tells us that DePugh started a pharmaceutical business called the Biolab Corporation in Independence in 1953 (p. 29). According to DePugh (October 20, 2006), the company produced both human and veterinary pharmaceutical products but about eighty percent of Biolab's business was veterinary products (See Appendix). The company mostly concentrated on producing a nutritional supplement for dogs called "Fidomin" (Jones, 1968, p. 29). Jones (1968) goes on to note: "Through the late '40s and the first several years of the '50s, DePugh was not especially preoccupied with political or ideological matters" (p. 29). This leads one to believe that during this period of his life, Bob DePugh was mostly concerned about succeeding in business and had little more concern about communism and world affairs than the average person of the day. However, the Biolab Corporation failed in 1955 for unknown reasons (p. 29). According to Schlatter (2003), the company failed because it was forced to pay back a large amount of backed taxes (p.41). However, this explanation of the company's failure seems to be pure speculation. Whatever the reason for Biolab's failure, it may have signaled an important change in the course of Bob DePugh's life.

According to Jones (1968), DePugh had his first brush with the law at about the same time his business failed in 1955. He was arrested in Kansas for passing bad checks after his business partners tipped off a bank in which DePugh had opened accounts under phony names. It seems clear that DePugh passed the bad checks in a desperate attempt to save Biolab. DePugh paid back the money he owed and all charges were dropped in 1956 (p. 30-31).

Following his first brush with the law, DePugh attended Washburn University for a short time while working as a salesmen selling prescription animal feed to veterinarians (Jones, 1968, p. 31). However, DePugh had not given up his dream of owning his own company and he restarted Biolab at 613 East Alton in Independence, Missouri, in 1959 (p. 31). 613 East Alton was an address that would be important in future Minutemen activities. This time DePugh's business would prove more successful. DePugh and his wife seemed to be the only employees of the business at the time and they kept busy producing Enzodime tablets that were purported to help extend the lifespan of dogs and keep them healthier in old age (p. 31).

According to Finch (1983), it is around this same time that DePugh, at the time a politically naïve businessman, made a small fortune with Biolab and finally had a chance to look at the world around him (p. 116). Apparently he did not like what he saw. He joined the John Birch Society although his membership would later be revoked for advocating extremist tactics. DePugh decided to become involved in the right wing cause (p.116-117). According to Jones (1968), DePugh made his first conservative political movement around 1959 when he took out an ad in the *Kansas City Star* to oppose firearm control legislation in the Missouri legislature (p. 32). According to Jones (1968), the ad read "History proves….that tyranny is the inevitable consequence when people forfeit their individual freedom" (p. 32). He also petitioned and held a meeting in Kansas City to oppose the legislation (p. 32). DePugh would continue to oppose gun control adamantly for many years.

According to Jones (1968), DePugh moved to Norborne, Missouri in 1960 after receiving a loan from the Norborne Development Company (p. 32-33). The DePugh family moved into a house located at 408 South Pine (p. 35). Norborne was, and is, a small town so a group of civic boosters in the community formed the Norborne Development Company during the 1950s to attract new businesses to the town. They offered a low interest loan of seven thousand five hundred dollars to DePugh so he could relocate Biolab to Norborne. Biolab was picked by the development company because they believed it had a good potential to succeed and grow. They also hoped it would provide employment for Norborne area residents. However, Norborne would not be ready for the attention it would gain from being the home of Robert DePugh's Minutemen (p. 33-34).

Chapter Three

The Little Town

Donald Janson (1961) quoted a Norborne, Missouri resident saying "He put us on the map" (p. 23). That was no doubt how many Norborne residents felt when they heard that their town was home to a right wing militia leader. According to Janson (1961), Norborne had a population of nine hundred fifty residents in 1961 (p.23). Janson (1961) also tells us that he could find no one in Norborne outside of the DePugh family who cared to be associated with the Minutemen. In fact, few residents knew of the Minutemen's existence until they read newspaper accounts of Minutemen activities in other states. Few residents of the small town seemed to have known DePugh well. He spent many hours working at Biolab and presumably spent a great deal of time concerning himself with Minutemen activities. As a result, he was rarely to be seen around town and did not fit in well in the small farming community. A resident of Norborne, Earl Wheeler, told Janson (1961): "He's a very peculiar sort of fellow. I can't make out whether he's a genius or a screwball" (p.23). That was surely the thought of many Norborne residents of the time, except those who dismissed the possibility that he was a genius and embraced the screwball image. However, after some initial shock at the news that the Minutemen leader inhabited their town, the Norborne residents seemed to take the Minutemen and their leader in stride. Hazel Linville told Janson (1961) "I think the whole thing is being taken as something of a joke here now" (p.23).

Jones (1968) seemed to have found a similar attitude among the townspeople during his visit to Norborne. A prominent Norborne resident, Mark Schweder, told Jones (1969) about a joke circulating the town suggesting that signs should be put up along the highways that read "Norborne, Home of the Minutemen" to attract tourists (p.352). Aside from joking, he did not find anyone willing to voice criticisms about DePugh and his family. Jones (1968) notes that one person "was quick to point out to me that DePugh had paid off nearly all of the loan and fully expected him to continue paying on it as long as necessary" (p. 34). Jones (1968) also found that the residents of the small town spoke favorably about DePugh's children and how they enjoyed reading, behaved themselves, and were liked by most people in the town (p. 34). Jones (1968) notes that the residents considered the children very patriotic, in the Minutemen sense of the word (p.34).

According to Jones (1968), Norborne also had [and continues to have] a small newspaper called the *Norborne Democrat-Leader*. He notes that the paper rarely contained any information about DePugh's Minutemen activities. Dorsey Hill, the editor at the time, explained to Jones (1968) that the paper refrained from printing information about the Minutemen to protect DePugh's children and his brother's family, who also lived in the area. The paper mostly concentrated on stories about the town not found in the larger newspapers. The larger newspapers did include stories about the Minutemen so there was no reason to include them in the local newspaper (p.33).

It seems that the residents tolerated DePugh and his Minutemen. According to Jones (1968), Minutemen from other parts of the country would often visit DePugh in Norborne. It seems unlikely that without at least a moderate amount of tolerance from local citizens, DePugh would have been able to carry out the controversial activities that would occur in the years that DePugh called Norborne his home. However, it does not seem likely that Norborne, or any great number of the town's residents, ever supported DePugh's Minutemen. According to Jones (1968), no evi-dence could be found that any of the area's residents joined the Minutemen (p.34-35).

Chapter Four

Formation of the Minutemen

After some discussion of Robert DePugh and the town that he called home during most of the Minutemen's existence, it is time to tackle the illusive subject of the Minutemen's formation. There are at least four different versions of how the Minutemen formed. All four of these versions will be discussed. It is important to note that all four versions reportedly originated from DePugh himself.

Finch (1983) tells us that DePugh first became interested in worldly affairs in the late '50s after succeeding in his pharmaceutical business. At this time DePugh joined the John Birch Society and became interested in contributing to the right wing cause. However, before contributing DePugh supposedly traveled the country and visited many right wing leaders to make sure he would be making his contributions to a worthy cause. DePugh did not like what he found (p. 116-117). According to Finch (1983), DePugh was "disappointed in almost every one of them. He found them lacking either personally or philosophically. Only one, a conservative minister from Aurora, Colorado, named Ken Goff, appealed to him as a man" (p. 117). After traveling the country, DePugh, disappointed in conservative leadership and thoroughly concerned about Communist takeover, decided to form the Minutemen to defend the United States from a coming Communist invasion (p. 117). According to Finch (1983), DePugh "adopted as their symbol the crossed hairs of a telescopic sight" (p. 117).

According to Carroll (October 31, 1966), the Minutemen concept originated during a duck hunting trip in 1959 (p. 40). Carroll (October 31, 1966) quoted DePugh: "We got to talking about how bad off the country would be in case of invasion and how such a group as ours could become a guerilla band" (p. 40). According to Carroll (October 31, 1966), "DePugh went on to head the organization" (p. 40).

Jones (1968) tells a very similar version of the Minutemen's formation. This version originated in a Minutemen publication titled "Minutemen-America's Last Line of Defense Against Communism" (p. 39). [The researcher was unable to obtain a copy of this publication.] According to Jones (1968), the organization evolved from a remark made by a duck hunter while building a blind in the summer of 1960 (p. 39). Jones (1968) quoted this remark: "Well, if the Russians invade us, we can come up here and fight on as a guerrilla band" (p. 39). This remark supposedly began a conversation about forming an organization to defend against a Communist invasion and eventually the group did form an organization which became known as the Minutemen (p. 39).

Jones (1968) goes on to tell a second version of the Minutemen's formation which DePugh told him during an interview in December 1966. According to this version, DePugh and some friends became admirers of Fidel Castro around 1958. DePugh's interest in Castro supposedly resulted from an article written by the revolutionary himself. However, eventually DePugh and his friends became aware that Castro was a Communist. DePugh and these friends then began discussing the problems of communism amongst each other and with others in Independence. Some of the other people they discussed the Communist problem with introduced them to anti-Communist literature. DePugh and his friends evidently became quite alarmed. The group is said to have studied communism thoroughly for a period of time and eventually there were ten people involved in this study and the discussions concerning communism. The group read literature from both the right and left wings on the subject (pp. 39-40). Jones (1968) notes:

> some in this group did belong to a duck-hunting club and did discuss such matters while sitting around in a duck blind....but if someone joked about fighting as a guerrilla band from the duck blind, "that certainly didn't mark the beginning of the organization." (p. 40)

After extensive study of communism the group started the Minutemen. Supposedly, the other charter members of the Minutemen formed the "Executive Council" of the Minutemen (p.40). According to Jones (1968), this was "a group of men to whom he [DePugh] has been answerable on major decisions as national Minutemen coordinator" (p. 40). Jones (1968) notes that DePugh was generally inconsistent in his statements concerning the "Executive Council" and that all the evidence pointed to there being no such council that governed DePugh (pp. 40-41).

In an interview with DePugh (October 20, 2006), he told the most recent version of how the Minutemen idea started. "Well it started in Independence, Missouri at a little coffee shop on Lexington Street a half a block west of the square" (See Appendix). DePugh (October 20, 2006) went on to describe a group of people who met for coffee at this little shop. He described them as a group of normal people. These people were all anti-Communist and they discussed communism but also talked about other things. DePugh (October 20, 2006) described the group talking about Castro fighting guerrilla warfare against Batista. The idea evolved that "if the Communists ever do invade this country we should reverse the situation on them and we should be prepared to fight a guerrilla war" (See Appendix). These discussions occurred around the late fifties but De-Pugh did not specify any certain date the Minutemen off-icially formed.

DePugh (October 20, 2006) went on to tell about some members of the group beginning to stockpile various items in case of a Communist invasion. He admitted that the stockpiling was probably where the group made their first mistake. Evidently the group began running into opposition when they began preparing for the Communist invasion they predicted in the future. According to DePugh (October 20, 2006) "We came to the conclusion that hell our own government has already gone Communist. They don't want us to defend individual freedom. The Second Amendment means nothing at all to them. The right to keep and bear arms is a façade" (See Appendix).

DePugh (October 20, 2006) notes that there were a couple duck hunters amongst the Independence discussion group. These hunters went on a hunting trip up to Swan Lake [a popular hunting destination in Missouri at the time]. According to DePugh (October 20, 2006), one of these men said "well….if worst comes to worst we'll just form our own guerrilla organization" (See Appendix) DePugh (October 20, 2006) goes on: "and so there was never really ever any one time that I really started the organization myself" (See Appendix). Around this time the group finally decided to form a guerrilla organization but it did not yet have a name.

DePugh (October 20, 2006) noted that he was moving his business to Norborne around this same time and was in the Norborne café when he came up with a name for the organization. While at the café he read a speech by John F. Kennedy who he believed was not yet President at the time. The speech called for a nation of minute men (See Appendix). According to DePugh (October 20, 2006), the fledgling organization was still debating whether or not it even needed a name. However, after reading the speech DePugh decided that "Minutemen" was a name that the organization's opposition could not find any fault with. However, DePugh (October 20, 2006) goes on to note that the opposition did find fault with the name (See Appendix). Nevertheless, according to DePugh (October 20, 2006), John F. Kennedy's speech is where the name Minutemen originated (See Appendix).

John F. Kennedy (January 29, 1961) did give the speech that DePugh (October 20, 2006) reported reading about but it was while he was president. He gave the speech for the Roosevelt Day Commemoration. President Kennedy (January 29, 1961) said:

> Today we need a nation of minute men; citizens who are not only prepared to take up arms, but citizens who regard the preservation of freedom as a basic purpose of their daily life and who are willing to consciously work and sacrifice for that freedom. The cause of liberty, the cause of America, cannot succeed with any lesser effort. (para. 6).

However, it seems doubtful the Bob DePugh's Minutemen were exactly what President Kennedy was calling for in this

Roosevelt Day message. The timeline of events in the Minutemen's history does allow for the possibility that Kennedy's speech was the origin of Minutemen's name. Also, no other more convincing explanation for the origin of the group's name can be found.

Ironically, a member of the Minutemen named Guy Bannister would later be suspected by conspiracy theorists in connection with President Kennedy's assassination. Lee Harvey Oswald put the address 544 Camp Street, New Orleans, on some flyers that supported Fidel Castro. 544 Camp Street happened to be the address of Guy Bannister's office. However, it is likely that Oswald used 544 Camp Street as a bogus address and no other connection between Oswald and Bannister has ever been made (Posner, 1993, pp. 136-137).

However the Minutemen originated and wherever their name came from, it is obvious that an organization named the Minutemen existed by October of 1961. According to Jones (1968), it was on October 21, 1961 that the Minutemen gathered for training exercises in Shiloh, Illinois and the press got their first look at the organization (pp.1-3). Information obtained from the FBI (November 3, 1966) under the Freedom of Information Act contains a report, which contains an appendix that notes the Minutemen were formed in June, 1960 (p. 5). According to this information the Minutemen may have existed more than a year before the Shiloh training exercise. However, it is necessary to discuss the early growth of the Minutemen before discussing the many events that followed the Minutemen's discovery in Shiloh. The early growth of the Minutemen is a topic that is shrouded in mystery.

According to Jones (1968), there were some minor variations among the stories concerning the early growth of the Minutemen. However, DePugh told one story in which an organization similar to the Minutemen contacted De-

Pugh. This group had significantly more military experience than the Minutemen. Presumably they were a group of reserve military officers. This group supposedly used the Minutemen as their front and attempted to recruit members for their own organization. However, DePugh indicated that their attempt backfired and the Minutemen grew very fast because they were the only organization of their type that advertised openly (pp. 41-42). While there is no way to know whether or not DePugh's story is true, it does seem almost certain that most of the Minutemen's early growth was due to their willingness to advertise openly in newspapers and distribute literature supporting their cause. It seems likely that the Minutemen were easy to contact because addresses appeared on most of their literature. Most members probably joined after reading about the Minutemen or hearing about them through the media. Most new recruits were individuals who were viciously anti-Communist and believed there was a real danger of Communist invasion. Presumably, they believed the Minutemen organization was a good cause that patriotic Americans should join. However, there is little factual information concerning why and how the Minutemen began to grow.

Chapter Five

Structure of the Minutemen

It is important to discuss the structure of the Minutemen in order to understand why the Minutemen would eventually run into so much opposition from society and the government. This opposition would be the primary cause of their downfall. According to Jones (1968), DePugh often claimed that he answered to the Minutemen's National Council. It is also widely accepted that DePugh was the Minutemen's sole national coordinator (p. 40). If the National Council did exist it would have been the top of the Minutemen's hierarchy. However, according to George and Wilcox (1996),

> In point of fact, a council existed on paper only, although some individuals were told they were "members." In 1966, however, DePugh said he had testified before a federal grand jury that the council didn't even exist, which confirmed the suspicions of various DePugh watchers. (p. 225)

According to Jones (1968), DePugh claimed the existence of such a council for the disinformation effect it would have on his enemies (p. 41). Jones (1968) quoted DePugh in reference to this disinformation effort: "This is one of the things I have absolutely got to keep my adversaries guessing about" (p. 41).

In absence of the existence of a National Council to govern the Minutemen, it seems certain the Robert DePugh was their highest leader. DePugh did step down from his leadership position for a short period of time in 1967 (Jones, 1968, p. 331). An article in the *New York Times* read: "Robert Bolivar DePugh announced today that he was resigning as national coordinator of the right-wing Minutemen. Henceforth, he indicated, it will operate in complete secrecy and completely underground" ("DePugh Quitting Minutemen Post," January 24, 1967, p. 34). However, he rejoined the Minutemen in May of 1967 because of what he described as internal problems in the organization ("DePugh Rejoins Minutemen," May 2, 1967, p. 40). As he was absent from leadership less than five months it can be assumed that Robert DePugh was the only important national leader the Minutemen ever had. Without a National Council, DePugh was at the top of the Minutemen hierarchy throughout all of the group's existence.

According to Hill (November 12, 1961), ten regional directors of the Minutemen operated below the national level. However, it does not seem that these were the same ten men that were supposedly on the Executive Council, which DePugh also claimed had ten members at one point. Hill (November 12, 1961) noted: "Mr. DePugh says, there is no 'chain of command' either upward or downward, on the theory that it is in the nature of guerilla units to operate independently" (p. 76). In an interview, DePugh (October 20, 2006) noted that there were state level coordinators but that there was no military style rank system in the organization (See Appendix). Jones (1968) also suggests that there were state-level leaders of the Minutemen (p. 64). These state leaders may have operated in addition to the regional directors or the position of state coordinator may have evolved from the regional director position as the organization grew. However, the absence of a chain of command in the Minutemen suggests that the regional and state coordinators were not responsible to DePugh and DePugh may not have had authority to give orders to the lower-level Minutemen.

According to Hill (November 12, 1961), DePugh indicated that there were unit leaders below the state coordinators. Each unit leader commanded a band of five to fifteen men. DePugh also indicated that the national organization required only the name and address of the unit leaders. The unit leaders did not even have to give their real name. In fact, anyone below the state level was encouraged to remain anonymous for security reasons (p. 76). In an interview DePugh (October 20, 2006), the former national coordinator concurred:

> Basically beneath the state level it was mostly a matter of people thought this idea up by themselves or maybe they heard, read something in the newspapers about it....and then wrote in and said, "How can I join?" We would put them in touch with people in that state, the coordinator or someone in that area, but we never did encourage them to self-identify themselves (See Appendix).

DePugh (October 20, 2006) also indicated that the Minutemen were loosely organized into small bands and that the closest they came to being nationally organized was with the state coordinators. Also, the Minutemen used numbers, instead of names, for identification purposes.

DePugh (October 20, 2006) indicated, "Each state had some one person who was sort of the leader of that state" (See Appendix).

According to Hill (1961), the Minutemen were loosely organized into small cells and the organization lacked structure, which hurt their potential to grow (p. 1). However, when asked if the loose organization style of the Minutemen eventually led to the government infiltration that caused the Minutemen's downfall, DePugh (October 20, 2006) said, "The fact that we were loosely organized is the only reason we survived as long as we did" (See Appendix).

George and Wilcox (1996) described a similar style of organization. They described the Minutemen being organized into small units which consisted of between five and twenty-five members. These units were not to know about each other. In fact, only state leaders were to know the identities of unit leaders. There were not supposed to be any records of individual members, even at the unit level. DePugh was only responsible for disseminating Minutemen literature and gaining publicity [which he excelled at] in order to recruit members at the unit level. The decentralized, or disorganized, nature of the Minutemen was supposed to make them more difficult to defeat during the Communist invasion as well as prevent infiltration (p. 223). However, according to George and Wilcox (1996):

> In reality, most Minutemen members were quickly known to authorities, often within days of their recruitment. The primary reason for this was their own indiscretion coupled with government infiltration and neutralization. The kind of individual attracted to such a marginal enterprise was often the typical compulsive extremist who had been active in other groups. (p. 223).

It seems that the Minutemen's loose organization style did lead to problems because small units of Minutemen, or even individual Minutemen, could act on their own volition without permission from their state coordinator or DePugh himself. However, it also seems that the organization could have used more anonymity, in addition to a vow of secrecy, to avoid the government infiltration that caused them immense problems. George and Wilcox (1996) noted that in addition to professional informants, individual Minutemen would commonly tell law enforcement anything they knew about the organization when they got into trouble (pp. 223-224).

The loose organization of the Minutemen most definitely led to one problem for researchers, but not for the Minutemen themselves. This problem is that nobody, including Bob DePugh, knows how many people were ever members of the Minutemen. There have been many estimates made concerning membership numbers. According to Jones (1968), DePugh told reporters at the 1961 Shiloh training session that there were about twenty-five thousand members (p. 3). Jones (1968) goes on to note that DePugh later admitted that there were probably not even six hundred members, and probably even fewer in 1961 (p. 3). DePugh would also make estimates of three hundred or four hundred on different occasions (p. 43). Jones (1968) made his own estimate concerning Minutemen membership:

> If a guess is in order--and it probably is not, for I could be disproved tomorrow--it would not amaze me to learn that there are as many as 1000 to 2000 active Minutemen in the country today. It would surprise me if there are many more than that. Many more undoubtedly have written letters of inquiry or applied for membership in the last six or seven

years, but most of them, it seems logical to assume, later departed. (p. 43)

An assistant district attorney for Queens, New York, later gave a different estimate, indicating national Minutemen membership in 1966 at more than ten thousand with several thousand very loyal active members (p. 311). This was surely an overestimate, even in 1966 during the Minutemen's peak years. The California attorney general believed there were between one hundred and six hundred members in his state during 1964 (p. 43). Jones (1968) goes on to note: "J. Edgar Hoover estimated the entire national membership in early 1968 at less than 500" (p. 43). However, it should also be noted that this estimate was made during the Minutemen's decline.

According to Schlatter (2003), peak membership in the Minutemen was between ten and fifteen thousand according to a 1978 issue of the *Kansas City Star*. This peak membership is said to have occurred during the mid 1960's (p. 43). Schlatter (2003) goes on to note that DePugh once estimated membership as being at least fifty thousand (p. 43). All of these numbers were probably overestimates.

George and Wilcox (1996) quoted DePugh's description of the Minutemen numbers as being around one hundred thousand on one occasion. One another occasion DePugh stated "membership close to 1,000,000 is possible in the near future" (p. 224). George and Wilcox (1996) go on to note many of the membership estimates already mentioned above. George and Wilcox (1996) then make their own estimate:

The actual number of genuine, active, committed Minutemen was in the neighborhood of two hundred, with a group of perhaps four hundred or more on the periphery at the organization's peak, most of whom only contributed money and received literature. Altogether perhaps as many as a thousand individuals had been "members" of the organization at one time or another, many for only a few years. (p. 225)

This estimate seems a bit low considering the amount of publicity the organization received during its peak prominence and the level of attention it received from federal authorities. However, it is almost impossible to make an accurate estimate concerning Minutemen membership numbers.

In an interview with DePugh (October 20, 2006), DePugh indicated how difficult it was to estimate how many people were ever active members of the Minutemen. According to DePugh (October 20, 2006), "It was hard to say where the membership started and where it ended" (See Appendix). DePugh (October 20, 2006) noted that there was not really a cutoff line between true members and sympathizers (See Appendix). DePugh (October 20, 2006) gave no estimate of Minutemen numbers during any period of the organization's existence in this interview.

Information obtained from the FBI (February 8, 1968) under the Freedom of Information Act included a report and the appendix attached to this report notes: "DePugh has stated the membership of the 'Minutemen' to be in excess of 35,000 members, however, confidential sources state this figure is greatly exaggerated and that a more true estimate would be between 800 and 2,000 members" (p. 3). Although the confidential source's estimate is surely more accurate than DePugh's, this number even seems a bit high for 1968.

Considering the great number of estimates that have been made concerning membership numbers in the Minutemen, it is impossible to determine which is the most accurate. It is quite likely that all of the aforementioned numbers are inaccurate to some degree and the true number of people who were once Minutemen will never be known. It seems wise to refrain from making estimates concerning Minutemen membership numbers, as any estimate would be almost pure speculation.

George and Wilcox (1996) described the advantage that not being able to determine membership numbers gave to DePugh and the Minutemen: "Clearly, the prospect of a large underground army was a haunting one and no one knew this more than DePugh himself. Psychologically speaking, the inflated figures represented a kind of shield for DePugh" (p. 224). Jones (1968) quoted DePugh concerning the Minutemen's advantage concerning the numbers mystery: "When somebody says we have no more than 2,000 members, I'm happy. When someone else says we have 35,000, I'm happy too. The very fact that people question this is an advantage" (p. 43). The numbers mystery may well have given an advantage to the Minutemen because nobody could know how big or strong of an underground army occupied the United States during the 1960s. No one could know how much, if any, threat the Minutemen posed to either communism or national security if they could not figure out how many Minutemen actually existed.

In addition to membership numbers, qualifications for membership are another interesting, but less mysterious, topic of discussion. According to Schlatter (2003), DePugh once stated that "any male United States citizen, loyal to the principles of liberty for which the [original] Minutemen fought, may join providing that he is at least fourteen years of age" (p.42). According to Schlatter (2003), DePugh also announced that membership in the Minutemen was open to anyone. However, Schlatter (2003) goes on to note that the only Minutemen who she knew of were white males (p. 43).

In an interview with DePugh (October 20, 2006), DePugh indicated that the Minutemen organization was open to more than just white males. He went on to note that around twenty percent of the Minutemen's membership was female (See Appendix). DePugh (October 20, 2006) also indicated that the Minutemen had several African American and Jewish members. However, these members were only allowed to play a limited role in the organization (See Appendix). Their duties primarily consisted of infiltrating and gathering information about organizations that other Minutemen members might not have access to. DePugh (October 20, 2006) went on to tell of one African American member who was very valuable because he was able to infiltrate all kinds of organizations (See Appendix). DePugh (October 20, 2006) did indicate that most people would be surprised by the number of ethnically Jewish members, although not all of them were members of the Jewish religion and many did not openly admit their Jewish ancestry (See Appendix). However, DePugh (October 20, 2006) made no statement that would question the generally held assumption that the organization was composed primarily of white males.

Aside from the question of racial and gender diversity in the Minutemen organization, little is known about specific qualifications for membership. There were probably few qualifications. However, it seems safe to assume that any potential member needed to be adamantly anti-Communist. Hill (November 12, 1961) notes that there was no physical fitness test required to join the Minutemen (p. 76). According to Hill (November 12, 1961), DePugh indicated that even a felony conviction did not prevent someone from joining the Minutemen. Essentially, membership was available to anyone (p. 76).

Information obtained from the FBI (July 31, 1966) under the Freedom of Information Act contains a report, which contains a copy of the Minutemen application form (pp 16a-16d). The application is four pages long and it requires some detailed information from applicants, including the potential member's social security number and a photograph. The application goes on to ask questions about the applicant's education, marital status, criminal record, and military service (p. 16b). The application also asks for references from the applicant's job, personal acquaintances, and other members they might know. It also asks the member to describe why they want to join the Minutemen (pp.16b-16c). Several other general questions are asked. The application also required an initial membership fee of ten dollars to be sent with the application. The ten dollar fee got the member a one year subscription to *On Target* and the *Minutemen Bulletin*. The monthly dues were three dollars in addition to the original ten (p. 16d). The end of the application includes what appears to be the Minutemen oath which has a signature and date line underneath it. The oath states: "To the restoration of our Constitutional Republic, to the defense of individual freedom and to the preservation of our American heritage, we pledge our lives, our fortunes and our sacred honor" (p. 16d).

The questions on the application form do not indicate whether a member will be automatically disqualified if they answer a certain way. However, it does seem safe to assume that a member could be rejected due to answers placed on the application form or if certain questions were left blank. The first page of the application does indicate that the purpose of the application is to prevent infiltration in the organization by its enemies. The application also states: "the following data is necessary if we are to accurately judge our new members' degree of sincerity and reliability" (FBI, July 31, 1966, p. 16a). The application was obviously used to screen out some applicants that the Minutemen did not judge to be suitable members. However, it seems unlikely that many members were rejected.

Despite the requirement of dues in the above-mentioned application, whether or not members were actually required to pay dues is a matter of some debate. Hill (1961) indicates that dues were optional (p. 76). In an interview, DePugh (October 20, 2006) also indicated that dues were not really required (See Appendix). According to Jones (1968) "Members' dues have been more or less on a pay-as-you-can basis with a minimum of $2 preferred each month, a maximum of $10 suggested" (p. 44). Jones (1968) goes on to note that dues were eventually raised. DePugh told Jones (1968) that members often failed to pay their dues (p. 44). Originally, the initial fee to join the Minutemen was only five dollars (p. 44). The sources indicate that although the organization did encourage members to pay dues, in reality they were not required.

Chapter Six

Minutemen Publications

After discussing the structure and membership of the Minutemen it seems proper to discuss the Minutemen's publications, as it is almost certain that most members were avid readers of DePugh's works. Robert DePugh was most likely the author of most Minutemen literature. His books will be discussed at this point as well. According to Jones (1968), *On Target* was a monthly publication of the Minutemen (p. 14). Jones (1968) describes *On Target* as follows: "it has provided a visual reminder of the nature of the Minutemen which no amount of patriotic euphemisms can erase. Decorating 'On Target's' masthead have been the cross hairs of a telescopic sight in the 'O' of the 'On'" (p. 14). According to Schlatter (2003), DePugh began publishing *On Target* in 1963 (p. 43). The pages of *On Target* often reported Communist threats to the United States and described how the United States government was infiltrated with Communists. The monthly newsletter often warned of possible threats to "American Patriots" and these "Patriots" were urged to buy guns (p. 43). George and Wilcox (1996) described DePugh as reporting a circulation of about two thousand copies for the newsletter, although that number cannot be verified (p. 224). DePugh (October 20, 2006) indicated that *On Target* was published from around 1955 until 1980, although he admitted he was not certain of those years (See Appendix). It does not seem likely that those numbers are correct because there is no evidence to indicate that the newsletter was ever published before or after the Minutemen's existence. *On Target* (January 1, 1966) indicates that the subscription rate for the newsletter was five dollars a year, which was included in Minutemen membership dues (p. 1) According to *On Target* (January 1, 1966), "We guarantee that all lawsuits filed against this newsletter will be settled out of court" (p. 1). This issue of the newsletter is a prime example of Minutemen anti-Communist rhetoric. A couple of quotations are in order. In reference to Cuba and Fidel Castro *On Target* (January 1, 1966) reports: "It has long been obvious that powerful forces within the United States government helped bring Fidel Castro to power in Cuba" (p. 1). *On Target* (January 1, 1966) also addresses a concern over atomic bombs as follows: "It is entirely possible that several dozen small atomic bombs have already been smuggled into this country and placed in strategic positions just waiting to be detonated by radio or time delay devices" (p. 8). *On Target* seems to have been the Minutemen's primary method of spreading their anti-Communist rhetoric as well as maintaining a sense of impending doom upon the members. If the situation had truly been as dim as the January 1, 1966 issue of *On Target* proclaimed, there was certainly reason for alarm. *On Target* (January 1, 1966) carried a slogan that seems very descriptive of the Minutemen's mindset: "Words Won't Win—Action Will" (p. 1).

Information obtained from the FBI (November 4, 1969) under the Freedom of Information Act contains a report, which contains a copy of a Minutemen publication titled *Mid Summer Bulletin* (p. 18). The bulletin is dated July, 1969 but is very hard to read due to the poor quality of the copy. However, it appears to contain information about structural changes within the Minutemen organization and a report form for members to fill out and send back to the national headquarters (p. 18-20). This bulletin may have been an issue of the *Minutemen Bulletin* referred to previously in the description of the Minutemen application form. If so, member dues would have also covered a one year sub-scription to this bulletin. The Minutemen also mailed out other letters on occasion for special reasons. A letter contained in the same FBI (November 4, 1969) report contains a letter to members from Ralph C. DePugh, [not to be confused with Robert DePugh's father, who was also named Ralph] the eldest of Robert DePugh's three sons, that announces that Ralph was the new national coordinator after Robert DePugh was imprisoned (p. 14). However, Ralph's term as national coordinator cannot be examined in depth as there is a scarcity of information concerning this period of the organization's existence. It can be assumed that the organization was essentially dis-banded during this period. Another report from the FBI (April 21, 1967) contains a letter in which DePugh resigns as national coordinator for the first time [not to be confused with his removal from power in 1969]. This letter places the date of DePugh's original resignation as January 21, 1967 (p. 15a). The same report from the FBI (April 21, 1967) contains a special bulletin from the mysterious Executive Council that announced a major reorganization for the Minutemen. It also announced that more emphasis would be put on local organizations and contact with the national level of the organization would be reduced greatly (p. 15e). Not much is known about these letters and bulletins as copies of them are rare. It is not known how widely or often these bulletins and letters were distributed. However, it does seem likely that they were at least mailed to all dues-paying members and that they played a large role in the Minutemen communication network.

In addition to *On Target* and the various newsletters, pamphlets, and bulletins that were most likely written by Robert DePugh, the Minutemen's leader also published at least three books. It should be noted that in addition to the three books that will be mentioned here, DePugh may have published two more books concerning biochemistry. However, neither book is relevant to the topic at hand. In addition, neither book could be located by the researcher.

DePugh's first book was *Blueprint for Victory*. According to Jones (1968), the book was first published around 1966 (p. 140). However, the earliest addition that could be obtained by the current researcher was the third edition published in 1970. There are numerous editions of the book, all out of print, but some editions can be obtained used from online booksellers for a significantly higher price than the original two dollars that appears on the cover of the third edition. In *Blueprint for Victory* DePugh (1970) essentially maps out what he believes to be the Communist threat and outlines what must be done to resist a Communist takeover of the United States. George and Wilcox (1996) describe *Blueprint for Victory* as DePugh's most successful publication (p. 227). According to George and Wilcox (1996), it is "a kind of superpatriotic manual on how to fight communism" (p. 227). DePugh (1970) describes the resistance he prescribes as being the duty of every patriotic American. DePugh (1970) explains the guerrilla tactics that were the Minutemen's trademark. According to DePugh (1970) "Given reasonable conditions of environment guerrillas can inflict extreme damage on an enemy and can ultimately lead to the defeat of forces far more numerous and better equipped than themselves" (p.

72). He goes on to give examples that include the Vietnam War, which he does not seem to support (p. 72). Throughout the one hundred and twenty-six pages of *Blueprint for Victory* DePugh (1970) describes the enemy's threat and the patriotic response in such a manner that one comes away from reading the book with the impression that if the situation had actually been as grave as DePugh believed, the Minutemen might have been a great organization. DePugh (1970) did not fill the pages of *Blueprint for Victory* with the racial slurs and supremacist rhetoric that is so common in other radical right-wing literature. It is from DePugh's books, such as *Blueprint for Victory*, that one gets the impression that the man is something more than your average extremist.

DePugh's second book, and the most readily available today, is *Can You Survive?*. There is only one known edition of *Can You Survive?* and it was published in 1973. The book is still in print although new copies of it can be difficult to find while less expensive used copies are readily available from most major online booksellers. The book is essentially a survival guide for Americans and their families in case of tyranny, presumably following a Communist invasion. It includes a fair amount of information previously published in Minutemen literature. DePugh (1973) describes survival techniques in different conditions such as the city, rural areas, and the wilderness (p. III). Although published after the Minutemen's decline, it is reminiscent of the organization. However, DePugh (1973) does not advocate the same level of violent resistance, or the same urgency of resistance, in *Can You Survive?* as he did in *Blueprint for Victory*. In fact, the chapter concerning resistance is limited to a few pages taken from an army manual concerning guerrilla warfare (pp 173-181). Although some of the information in *Can You Survive?* might be useful in surviving a Communist invasion, or the tyrannical government that might result from such an invasion, the book is not a call-to-arms for patriotic Americans as *Blueprint for Victory* was. However, once again one gains the impression from *Can You Survive?* that DePugh is something more than your average extremist.

Beyond the Iron Mask is DePugh's third and most un-characteristic book. The first, and only know edition of the book was published in 1974 by the Salon Publishing Company in Norborne, Missouri. The address of the Salon Publishing Company is 111 S. Pine Street. As this address is that of a building owned by DePugh in Norborne it is safe to assume that the Salon Publishing Company was one of DePugh's many enterprises, perhaps formed only to publish *Beyond the Iron Mask*. *Beyond the Iron Mask* is out of print and somewhat difficult to find.   In this book DePugh (1974) departs from his normal warnings of Communist invasion and tyrannical governments. According to George and Wilcox (1996), "While in prison DePugh wrote a surprising book, *Behind* [sic] *the Iron Mask*, in which he advocated measures for liberal prison reform. He also became a strong advocate of rehabilitation—somewhat out of character for a hide-bound right-winger" (p. 230). DePugh (1974) described his ideas for prisoner rehabilitation:

> He [the prisoner] may come to prison identifying himself as a clever thief, tripped up by bad luck, or as a man "born to lose," predestined to failure and doomed by fate to a lifetime in prison, or perhaps as one whose success has been denied by the prejudice or greed of others. He needs to shake off this old identity and find a new one that is compatible with his needs, his capabilities, and legal conduct within a free society. This means careful planning before his release, continued supervision after his release and a psychological bridge between the two (p. 394).

According to George and Wilcox (1996), DePugh also inserts his usual view of social Darwinism into the book but shifts again "to a critique of law enforcement practices that would do credit to an ACLU attorney" (p. 230). However, DePugh (1974) does not abandon all of his old Minutemen-era philosophies on overbearing government in *Beyond the Iron Mask*. DePugh (1974) advocates his belief that there are a great number of political prisoners in America's prison system, although he believes they are always convicted of some crime that is not political to cover up the confinement of persons for political reasons (p. 129). DePugh (1974) also notes that the average intelligence of federal prisoners is greater than the general public might believe it is. George and Wilcox (1996) conclude: "There is far more to DePugh than originally meets the eye. He is no ordinary right-wing nut case" (p. 230). Finch (1983) makes a similar conclusion concerning DePugh: "He is a thinker, a theoretician, of the sort usually associated with the intellectual left. Nobody else has set down so clearly the philosophy of the right wing movement—its ideals, its goals, its place in the national life" (p. 115). Finch (1983) goes on to praise DePugh's writing ability (p. 115). This conclusion is not difficult to make after reading the four hundred and twenty-seven pages of DePugh's longest work. DePugh is a very complex and interesting person.

Chapter Seven

Purpose of the Minutemen

After taking an in depth look at the structure of the Minutemen, including their membership and the publications that many members undoubtedly read, it is time to take a look at the Minutemen's purpose. The purpose of the Minutemen is far more complex than simply stating that they were an anti-Communist organization. Finch (1983) described the Minutemen as an underground resistance system that got national publicity during its infancy through training exercises that involved military weapons (p. 26). According to Finch (1983), DePugh labeled the Minutemen a "counterinsurgency group" (p. 26). Others have called the group subversive or revolutionary (p. 26). George and Wilcox (1996) describe the Minutemen's purpose as being a guerrilla organization that could fight the Communists in the event of an invasion (p. 221).

It is well known that fighting guerrilla warfare against a Communist invasion was the Minutemen's proclaimed purpose. However, to do this they needed to preserve their right to bear arms, which according to

DePugh (October 20, 2006), was in great danger (See Appendix). The Minutemen, like most right wing groups, were fierce protectors of the Second Amendment in addition to being fiercely anti-Communist. DePugh (1970) described the real purpose of the Second Amendment as follows: "To provide the citizens a means by which they could, if necessary, protect themselves against their own government" (p. 68). DePugh (1970) argued that if this was an extreme view then the founding fathers must also be labeled extremists because their sole purpose in protecting the right to bear arms was so the citizens could in turn protect themselves from a tyrannical government (pp. 68-69). According to DePugh (1970), since every government in history had become oppressive over time the founding fathers believed that the Second Amendment would provide the people one more way to resist tyranny (p. 69). DePugh (1970) notes: "This was the real reason for the second amendment—to give the people one last 'guarantee' by which they could protect themselves from their own government—when all other measures fail—by force of arms" (p. 71). According to Hill (November 12, 1961), DePugh used the First and Second Amendments to defend the Minutemen's training activities. Firearms were commonly used or at least displayed during the training exercises (p. 76). In the absence of fully automatic firearms, the Minutemen's activities did fall within the limits of the members' Constitutional rights. It was very important for the Minutemen to support a strict interpretation of the Second Amendment. This was not just because they believed in the right to keep and bear arms, but because it meant that their activities were legal. The organization gained some sense of legitimacy if their activities were constitutionally protected.

In addition to the purpose of protecting the United States from communism and maintaining the right to bear arms, which DePugh outlined in *Blueprint for Victory*, the Minutemen have been accused of being a white supremacist organization. They have also been misinterpreted as aiming to takeover the United States government, either through political domination or violent overthrow. Robert DePugh has also been accused of organizing the Minutemen for the purpose of personal financial gain or being a Communist himself. These accusations, and their truthfulness, or untruthfulness, will be examined next.

The first topic to consider is whether or not the Minutemen were a white supremacist organization. It seems that because so many right-wing extremists groups are outspokenly racist, the Minutemen have gotten lumped into the white supremacist category. According to Schlatter (2003), DePugh once "stated flatly that 'Negroes' are not capable of voting intelligently and he dismissed African American participation in government as part of a larger Communist subversion" (p. 44). However, Schlatter (2003) also notes that this racism was rare for DePugh and that Minutemen literature is not generally racist (p. 44, 164).

DePugh did have a tendency to be involved with other leadership figures on the radical right and thus he was surrounded by racists and anti-Semites. Roy Frankhouser was one such figure. According to Jones (1968), Frankhouser was a Grand Dragon of the Pennsylvania branch of the Ku Klux Klan (p. 359). According to George and Wilcox (1996), DePugh made Frankhouser a regional coordinator for the Minutemen in the Pennsylvania area during the mid 1960s (p. 232). Jones (1968) notes that in Pennsylvania during 1966, Klan membership also included membership in the Minutemen organization (p. 359). Information obtained from the FBI (December 30, 1966) under the Freedom of Information Act contains a report which indicates that Roy Frankhouser was a leader of the Free Corps. The Free Corps reportedly promoted policies and programs of the American Nazi Party, the Minutemen, and the United Klans of America (p. 3). Another FBI (April 21, 1967) report contains information from a confidential informant that indicates "the Minutemen are a secretive military organization, who are anti-communist and would appear to be somewhat along the thinking lines of the United Klans of America but are not as outspoken (p. 4). This information suggests that the Minutemen and the United Klans of America did cooperate. However, George and Wilcox (1996) suggest that Roy Frankhouser was a government informant who infiltrated all varieties of right-wing organizations (pp. 232-233). If Frankhouser was a government informant then he may have intentionally connected the Minutemen and the Klan himself without the cooperation or even the approval of DePugh. George and Wilcox (1996) note: "Although DePugh surrounded himself with racists and anti-Semites, many people who know him said he was never particularly outspoken against blacks and Jews....His primary preoccupation was always Communist subversion and disloyalty" (p. 241). This leads one to believe that although the Pennsylvania Minutemen may have had a white supremacist purpose, to label the entire Minutemen organization as white supremacist would be an overgeneralization.

Jones (1968) notes that George Lincoln Rockwell, leader of the American Nazi party, commented favorably concerning the Minutemen's stated purpose. He also indicated that he had lost some members and financial support to the Minutemen. DePugh confirmed that some former American Nazis had joined the Minutemen because they became disillusioned with the American Nazi Party. As such, Rockwell had no reason to support the Minutemen. Rockwell did indicate that he did not support the Minutemen's tactics, which according to him included the possession of illegal weapons by almost every member (p.

111). There is no evidence of cooperation between the Minutemen and the American Nazi Party, or that DePugh and Rockwell cooperated. However, since some people were members of both organizations, although perhaps not at the same time, the misconception could be made that the organizations shared similar anti-Semitic attitudes. Jones (1968) also noted that most Minutemen members would be extremely insulted if they were labeled fascists (p. 111).

When asked whether or not the Minutemen was a racist organization, DePugh (October 20, 2006) replied: "That was never the intent from the organization's point of view" (See Appendix). From this statement and the above-mentioned information one gets the impression that although the Minutemen was not a white supremacist organization itself, the Minutemen was full of white supremacists. Jones (1968) indicates that even Wally Peyson, one of DePugh's most loyal members, engaged in a lot of racist language (p. 197). It is debatable whether or not an organization that is primarily composed of racists is automatically a racist organization, even if that is not its proclaimed purpose.

The question of whether or not part of the Minutemen's purpose was to takeover the United States government is a tricky one. The Minutemen believed that the United States government was deeply infiltrated with Communists. DePugh (1970) notes: "During the past thirty years the legal government of the people has been taken over by the foreign ideology of a socialist bureaucracy" (p. 81). In an interview DePugh (October 20, 2006) noted that in the Minutemen's early years he, and others, came to the conclusion that the government had already gone Communist (See Appendix). According to Hill (November 12, 1961), DePugh indicated that Congressmen and Rep-resentatives could be Communists. Many people could be Communists without even knowing it (p. 76). According to

Jones (1968), the Minutemen focused on Communist infiltration in the Kennedy administration before the President was assassinated (p. 107). The Minutemen seemed to believe there was a hidden Communist government in the United States that would eventually take over the current democratic government (p. 122). The organization claimed to know of approximately sixty-five thousand Communists and "fellow travelers" in the United States (p. 122). Twenty-five or thirty persons who were supposedly known to have been members of the hidden Communist government were marked for assassination. The Minutemen knew who these people were because they had infiltrated the Communist Party. DePugh acknow-ledged that the Minutemen had also been infiltrated by Communists but that they knew who these infiltrators were. The known Communists were not to be assassinated until the hidden government took power (p. 122). Presumably, the Minutemen did not think it was possible to stop the hidden Communist government from taking power, but they did believe they could reclaim power from the Com-munists after they took over. According to Jones (1968), DePugh and the Minutemen labeled a person a Communist if they consistently took actions that followed the Com-munist line (p. 123). This is by no means a definite way to determine who actually belonged to the Communist party, and was part of the hidden Communist government. This caused the problem of knowing when the government had become Communist, and when Minutemen activities could begin. According to Jones (1968), DePugh believed the takeover would occur between 1984 and 1991 (p. 123). Jones (1968) quoted DePugh: "The anti-Communist revolt will come when the country is so indisputably Communist that everyone over seven years old will know it" (p. 123). However, even this explanation left considerable interpret-tation for individual members to decide when the war against the Communists should begin.

Finch (1983) quoted DePugh as follows: "We also decided that a pro-American government could no longer be established by normal political means [and that] any further effort, time or money spent in trying to save our country by political means would be wasted...." (p. 124). This certainly sounds like a threat to the elected government as it was in 1964. However, Finch goes on to note: "He [DePugh] must have known that organized military action by civilians is pointless and suicidal as long as elected government exists here" (p. 125). Finch (1983) instead suggests that DePugh's aim for the Minutemen may have been psychological warfare against whoever DePugh thought was a Communist (p. 125). According to Jones (1968), DePugh advocated psychological warfare (p. 357). This may have been especially true in the Minutemen's later years. According to Jones (1969), the Minutemen set off propaganda cannons across the country in 1968 or 1969 carrying Minutemen messages (pp. 364, 368-369).

In retrospect it does not seem that the Minutemen ever intended an armed takeover of the elected United States government. As Finch (1983) noted, they must have known it would have been suicidal. However, it does seem that they had every intention of resisting the Communist government that they were sure would eventually take over and oppress the American people. DePugh and his Minutemen seem to have always been preparing for a day that never came, or has not yet come, as DePugh might put it. There seems little doubt that the Minutemen were a dangerous organization as a result of their loose organization. Any member could have potentially decided for himself that the time for armed resistance had come and commit any number of terrible acts. However, if the United States had been in grave danger of a Communist takeover, and their day for armed resistance had come, they might be regarded in a totally different light today.

Another topic to be considered is the political aim of the Minutemen. According to George and Wilcox (1996), "DePugh launched his Patriotic Party, which was to be the political arm of the Minutemen" (p. 227). DePugh (October 20, 2006) indicated that the Patriotic Party was formed because the Minutemen came to realize that if they could not win against the Communists politically, they would not be able to win at all (See Appendix). Epstein and Forster (1967) note the Patriotic Party was designed by DePugh to unite radical right-wing organizations. Members of the party were to infiltrate the two dominant parties (p. 45). They also indicate that the Patriotic party was supposed to be the political organization of the Minutemen (p. 45). According to Epstein and Forster (1967), DePugh did not believe that a political party could save the United States from communism by using conventional means and that the dominant political parties did not have the strength to regain power from the Communists, as he believed the Communists already had enough control of the government that it was impossible to regain power purely through the electoral process (p. 48). This certainly leads to speculation as to why DePugh would ever have formed the Patriotic Party since he must have known it was doomed to fail. Perhaps DePugh believed the Patriotic Party could gain power through unconventional means such as armed action.

Whatever the case, the Patriotic Party was closely associated with the Minutemen organization and deserves discussion. However, it does not seem likely that that the Patriotic Party was intended to become a dominant political party through legitimate means. DePugh (1970) indicated "In 1972 we will make a one-time try at the presidency. That must be a do-or-die effort. No party can possibly put a real patriot in the White House before that date and our free Republic cannot last much longer" (p. 98). However, DePugh (1970) notes in the appendix that this message, which first appeared in the original edition of *Blueprint for Victory*, was not possible in 1972 but that the Patriotic Party must keep trying (pp. 120-121). Even DePugh seemed to have realized that the Patriotic Party could not possibly become a dominant political party in the near future.

George and Wilcox (1996) note that the Patriotic party was formed in 1966 and lasted only a few years (p. 227). DePugh (1970) outlined the platform for the Patriotic Party in *Blueprint for Victory*. According to Schlatter (2003), national conventions for the Patriotic Party were held in Kansas City for at least two years, 1966 and 1967. The conventions were held at the U-Smile Motel and the Town House Motor Inn respectively. Although these conventions never attracted the crowds the Patriotic Party leaders hoped for, they did manage to nominate George Wallace, an Alabama segregationist, as their presidential candidate in 1967 to run for president in 1968 (pp. 45-47). According to Jones (1968), William Penn Patrick was the Patriotic Party's vice-presidential candidate, although the party later withdrew Patrick's nomination for unknown reasons, possibly because he did not accept the nomination or because he was not raising any money for the campaign (pp. 288, 290-291). Jones (1968) noted DePugh was not particularly thrilled with Wallace but he was the best man for the nomination. The Patriotic Party did not withdraw Wallace's nomination (pp. 290-291). After the Patriotic Party's candidate was defeated not much more is known about the party. They seem to have faded away with the Minutemen in the late early 1970s. There seems to be no evidence that the Patriotic Party ever intended to take power through armed action. However, it does not seem likely that many members would have ever believed it possible for the party to elect a president by 1972. The Patriotic Party was most likely a last ditch effort by DePugh and the Minutemen to form a legitimate organization to fight communism. They must have hoped that the party would be accepted by the general public. However, the Patriotic Party was too closely associated with the Minutemen and thus gained its own dismal reputation.

There are two final topics concerning the Minutemen's purpose that merit discussion. The first is the accusation that DePugh formed the Minutemen for his own financial gain, and thus the purpose of the Minutemen was solely to make DePugh money. This second is that DePugh was a Communist himself.

According to Jones (1968), DePugh maintained that operating funds for the Minutemen organization were collected through dues and contributions. Dues were relatively low, between two and three dollars per month. DePugh also claimed that the largest contribution the organization ever received was five hundred dollars (p. 44). As the Minutemen always insisted on contributors and members sending cash, there is no reliable way to know how much money the Minutemen received through contributions. However, according to Jones (1968), one young woman who worked for the Minutemen as a secretary in 1965 said the organization received about two hundred dollars through the mail one day (p. 44). Even in the mid-1960s this was not a particularly large amount of money. According to Jones (1968), the Minutemen's expenses included printing fees and postage (p. 45). Jones (1968) also notes "One big organizational expense in evidence is paying lawyers' and bail bondsmen's fees for DePugh and others who have run afoul with the law (p. 45). These legal expenses were quite large, and considering the amount of mailing the Minutemen did, those expenses must have been large as well. There is also the possibility that the Minutemen had a few full-time employees who were paid, which would have been quite expensive. DePugh solicited contributions and sold literature almost every opportunity he had. However, Jones (1968) notes that DePugh owed people money and was investigated by the IRS for using Biolab profits to finance the Minutemen. DePugh did not live extravagantly (p. 46). Jones (1968) concludes:

> To all appearances, DePugh has not profited financially from his Minutemen efforts. If anything, they may have hurt him.... DePugh seems to have devoted far more time to the Minutemen than he has to Biolab and presumably could have helped build up the company's business had he spent all his time on it. (p. 46).

Jones (1968) also notes that DePugh took many risks as national coordinator of the Minutemen, and that most people would not take those risks for money (p. 47).

George and Wilcox (1996) concur that extremist groups are rarely just confidence games to make money (p. 225). According to George and Wilcox (1996) "The out of pocket cost to DePugh of his various activities almost certainly exceeded any funds coming in, not to mention the value of the time taken away from a relatively profitable business and devoted to his numerous right-wing projects" (p. 225).

When asked in an interview if he was in the Minutemen for the money, DePugh (October 20, 2006) replied "Whenever anybody says that ask them 'How?'....They don't understand the situation" (See Appendix). DePugh (October 20, 2006) also indicated that his Minutemen activities nearly ruined Biolab, although it never went bankrupt. According to DePugh (October 20, 2006), "I could've been a millionaire several times over if I'd of just stuck to business" (See Appendix). DePugh is not a millionaire today, and from his lifestyle it does not seem at all likely that he ever was. All the available evidence suggests that the Minutemen and the Patriotic Party hurt DePugh financially, especially in the later years. There is nothing to suggest that Robert DePugh ever made any money from the Minutemen, any statements contradictory to this must be pure speculation.

Another theory, even less likely than the Minutemen being a profitable organization for DePugh, is that DePugh was a Communist. If DePugh had been a Communist, he might have formed the Minutemen to distract attention from Communist activities and to cause public disapproval of anti-Communist organizations. The Minutemen's counterproductive actions and DePugh's often contradictory statements might be taken as evidence that he was a Communist in disguise. However, DePugh (1970) states his own case against this theory as follows:

> For many months now, I've been proving my loyalty to the patriotic conservative movement and the sincerity of my convictions by the surest means I know—by continuing to fight for the cause of liberty in spite of handicaps that few can comprehend—day after day, week after week, month after month—in a solitary confinement cell, in the maximum security building, behind the forty foot high walls of Leavenworth Penitentiary. (pp. 122-123).

This statement is hard to argue with. If DePugh was a Communist it does not seem rational that he would have risked spending numerous years in prison promoting a right-wing organization that would only hopefully end up aiding the left-wing. Surely if DePugh was actually a

Communist, he could have formed the Minutemen and distracted attention from Communists without risking prison time, and even his own life.

According to Jones (1968), DePugh admitted that it was difficult to convince a person he was not a Communist if they believed strongly that he was one. However, DePugh pointed out that his children were all anti-Communist and that it would be difficult for his whole family to deceive the other Minutemen (pp. 48-49). According to Jones (1968), DePugh also pointed out that the Minutemen trained people in guerrilla warfare and produced dangerous patriots who were viciously anti-Communist. It would not make sense to train anti-Communists to make them dangerous men if DePugh was a Communist. If not for joining the Minutemen, most of the members would have posed little threat to the Communists (p. 49). However, Jones (1968) notes that DePugh may have trained these people and gained publicity for the militant activities to cause problems for other right-wing organizations (p. 50). Although the available information suggests that DePugh may have discredited the right wing to some extent, and the militant right a bit more, it does not seem that he discredited anyone too much except for the Minutemen themselves. Surely if DePugh was a Communist trying to discredit right-wing groups he could have found a better way to do it. Also, he surely could have found a way that involved less personal risk than was associated with the Minutemen and his activities therein.

Chapter Eight

Controversy

One very important aspect of the Minutemen organization is the constant political and social controversy that it created throughout its existence. It was never an organization willing to make compromises or get along with other organizations, either on the radical right or elsewhere. The Minutemen criticized government and public figures often, and although this was no crime, it did create a lot of enemies from people who might not otherwise have had any adverse opinion concerning the Minutemen. However, one of the Minutemen's most controversial steps was threatening public figures, which did cause them a lot of problems. According the an article in the *New York Times* titled "Minutemen Cleared of Anti-U.S. Actions" (February 4, 1964), Henry B. Gonzalez, a Texas Democrat, asked for an investigation into the Minutemen. The reason for the investigation was "the Minutemen, in a publication, had issued 'a thinly veiled threat against me [Gonzalez] and my other colleagues who voted against the increased House Committee on Un-American Activities appropriation'" (p.

27). However, the article notes that Attorney General Robert Kennedy reported that the investigation found no prosecutable offenses by the Minutemen but that the Attorney General's office would continue to monitor the Minutemen. DePugh's reaction to this was "If Robert Kennedy can't find anything we've done illegally, it certainly is not because he has not tried" ("Minutemen Cleared of Anti-U.S. Actions", February 4, 1964, p. 27). According to Jones (1968), twenty Congressmen, including Gonzalez, were threatened in the March 15, 1965 issue of *On Target* (p. 12). According to Jones (1968), the threat was a warning stated as follows "Cross hairs are on the backs of your necks" (p. 12). Information obtained from the FBI (July 31, 1968) contains a report with a copy of a sticker distributed by the Minutemen which contains some of the same wording as the threat against the Congressmen (p. 29). The wording on the threatening sticker follows [it is included in its entirety for full effect]:

> See the old man at the corner where you buy your papers? He may have a silencer equipped pistol under his coat. That extra fountain pen in the pocket of the insurance salesman who calls on you might be a cyanide gas gun. What about your milk man? Arsenic works slow but sure. Your auto mechanic may stay up nights studying booby traps. These patriots are not going to let you take their freedom away from them. They have learned the silent knife, the strangler's cord, the target rifle that hits sparrows at 200 yards. Traitors beware. Even now the cross hairs are on the back of your necks (FBI, July 31, 1968, p. 29).

This sticker and the warning towards the Congressmen depict the threatening nature of the Minutemen well. The

Minutemen used the cross hairs symbol and threatening propaganda such as this against what they believed was the Communist enemy. Of course, these threats alarmed a great many people, especially those who were being threatened.

In addition to threatening public officials, DePugh (1970) took a more subtle step against supposed Communists and Communist sympathizers in *Blueprint for Victory*. DePugh (1970) listed the names of seventy-four well known people who belonged to Communist front organizations (pp. 34-35). Among the names were Lucille Ball, Charlie Chaplain, Frank Sinatra, Humphrey Bogart, Rita Hayworth, and Katherine Hepburn (p. 34-35). While DePugh (1970) made no direct threat to these persons, it could be considered a threat in and of itself to be named as a Communist or Communist sympathizer in *Blueprint for Victory*. After all, this publication was almost a manual for violent resistance against Communism.

The Minutemen's threatening nature led to an outcry against the Minutemen. One of the most important elements of this outcry was the Reuther Memorandum. According to George and Wilcox (1996), the Reuther Memorandum was a document formulated by Walter and Victor Reuther. Walter was president of the United Auto Workers (UAW) at the time. Walter's brother Victor was also an important figure in the UAW. Attorney General Robert Kennedy asked the Reuthers for advice concerning how to deal with, or more accurately, how to get rid of the Minutemen and other worrisome political groups. The Reuthers responded with what has become known as the Reuther Memorandum (pp. 222-223).

According to Finch (1983), the Reuther Memorandum was dated December 19, 1961 and in addition to the Minutemen it marked other radicals such as Billy James Hargis, Fred Schwartz's Christian Anti-Communist Crusade, and the John Birch Society for federal attention. The document was supposed to be confidential, but somehow the press got a hold of it. The Memorandum suggested ways to use presidential political influence to demolish these right-wing movements (p. 119). Finch (1983) notes: "The document is not one of the nobler legacies of the Kennedy administration….it is disturbingly similar in approach to the "enemies list" that would be drafted in the Nixon White House a decade later" (p. 119). According to Finch (1983), the Reuther Memorandum made several suggestions for dealing with the groups named as they would not be easy to get rid of. Finch (1983) notes:

> It suggests, among other tactics, the revocation of tax-exempt status for some right-wing groups; IRS scrutiny of right-wingers' tax returns and of contributions by businesses to the offending organizations; use of the Federal Communications Commission to discourage the free time being given to right-wing speakers; and FBI infiltration of right-wing groups. (p. 119)

According to Finch (1983), the Reuthers made several suggestions to Robert Kennedy about actions to take against the right-wing (pp. 119-120). According to Finch (1985), the fourth of five suggested actions on the list read as follows: "The Administration should take steps to end the Minutemen" (p. 120). This was most likely the national reaction DePugh was hoping for when he began antagonizing liberals in government. DePugh and his Minutemen got huge amounts of publicity from the Reuther Memorandum, which was just what the group needed to attract members. Finch (1983) tells us "the Minutemen now were certifiably dangerous, worthy of the most stringent measures that the attorney general could bring to bear against them" (p. 120). According to Finch (1983), DePugh knew how to capitalize from the outrage of government officials against the Minutemen. DePugh most likely believed, perhaps accurately, that he had become an important extremist figure in America.

Jones (1968) notes that whenever the Reuther Memorandum is spoken of on the Radical Right, it is "spoken with harsh contempt" (p. 69). According to Jones (1968) the radical right believed the Reuther Memorandum proved that there was a liberal conspiracy bent on destroying various right wing organizations, most specifically those mentioned in the document (p. 70). A good example of this is a book titled *The Reuther Memorandum: Its Applications and Implications* by William E. Mallett (1965). This book reprints the Memorandum in full and inserts comments criticizing the Reuthers, the Kennedy Administration, and suggesting Communist motives within the left. It should be noted that the Reuther Memorandum does seem like proof that liberals were cooperating in an effort to destroy, or at least diminish the influence of the radical right. However, the radical right was often guilty of conspiring to minimize left wing influence as well. If the right believed there was a conspiracy against them they were most likely correct, but they were also guilty of conspiring against political opponents themselves. Jones (1968) also states, "It [The Reuther Memorandum] undoubtedly delighted DePugh, however, for it tended to upgrade the status of the Minutemen substantially" (p. 70). Jones (1968) quotes the Reuther Memorandum concerning the suggested action against the Minutemen. The passage is as follows: "It is not known whether the Minutemen will grow or whether they will fade out of the picture. They do, however, represent a dangerous precedent in our democracy" (p. 70). Considering the rather small size of the Minutemen organization when the Reuther Memorandum was written, the organization did receive a disproportionate amount of attention. This only served to give the Minutemen greater publicity and help the Minutemen. It did not hurt them. According to Jones (1968) Victor Reuther later claimed that the Minutemen were not given a disproportionate amount of consideration in the document (pp 70-71). However, the document speaks for itself because it singles out the Minutemen while giving only passing notice to larger organizations which were better known at the time. Jones (1968) quoted DePugh's response to why the Minutemen were singled out as follows: "Because the Minutemen represent what the Communists fear the most—that the Communists' own methods might be used against them" (p. 71). The Minutemen were at least feared by liberals, if not Communists, as evident by the amount of liberal politicians who denounced the Minutemen in 1961 and the years to follow.

An impressive list of officials spoke out against the Minutemen in 1961 to further publicize the growing group. Among these officials were Governor Otto Kerner of Illinois, Governor "Pat" Brown of California, Jacob Javits (Senator, New York), Stanley Mosk (Attorney General, California), and John Shelley (Congressmen, California) (p. 118). President Kennedy never specifically mentioned the Minutemen. However, According to Finch (1983), President Kennedy did mention "armed bands of civilian guerrillas that are more likely to supply local vigilantes than national vigilance," which could certainly include the Minutemen (p. 119). According to Jones (1968), DePugh replied to President Kennedy's speech "assuring the President that his organization was not trying to raise a private army 'or take any other action which is in conflict with the principles of our constitutional republic'" (p. 69). President Kennedy's January 1961 speech calling for a nation of Minute Men had already backfired by the time he made the speech against extremist political groups in November 1961.

According to a *New York Times* article titled "A Coast Ban Sought on Rightest Militia" (January 7, 1964), California Attorney General Stanley Mosk continued his assault on the Minutemen after 1961. According to the article Mosk said "he would push for a state law banning the Minutemen and other private military groups" (p. 39). Mosk also sought tougher laws on firearm control to make the Minutemen less dangerous (p. 39) However, a law against the Minutemen might have been difficult to enforce, as members could always deny they belonged to the organization. Since few membership records were kept it would have been difficult to prove otherwise.

Another *New York Times* article titled "Senator Young Asks Curb on Minutemen" (February 5, 1965) described some of the adamant opposition the Minutemen provoked and received from government officials. Senator Stephen Young, an Ohio Democrat, described the Minutemen as a "band of psychotics", "demagogues of the extreme right", and "sandlot witchhunters" (p. 15). Senator Young suggested action against the Minutemen by the U.S. Department of Justice (p.150).

Perhaps the Minutemen's greatest success during their relatively short existence was their ability to antagonize liberal politicians. If the Minutemen did not like what a politician said they criticized him incessantly. Of course this was their First Amendment Right. Although Minutemen activities, such as making threats to various people, fell outside their plethora of rights, by far most Minutemen activities in the early years of the organization were completely legal. In fact most were even protected by the Constitution, which the Minutemen reported to be defending. Most Minutemen activities did not include training with fully automatic weapons and explosives. Minutemen activities generally consisted of members' practicing their right of free speech. When Minutemen activities did include weapons they were most often legal. Otherwise the Minutemen could have all been arrested and imprisoned long before they had a chance to become a prominent right-wing organization. This may have been what frustrated the left the most in the early years. They were unable to get rid of a radical organization that was at least annoying, if not dangerous, because they were not really doing anything illegal. However, as the Minutemen grew so did their illegal activities. Ultimately, the decision to employ more extreme tactics, and cross the limits of the law, is what led to trouble for the Minutemen.

At this point it is necessary to note that the media had a major impact on the Minutemen by publicizing the organization. According to George and Wilcox (1996) the Minutemen made a large portion of their impact through the media (p. 222). If not for the media, very few people would have ever heard of the Minutemen. The media put the Minutemen and Norborne, Missouri on the map. According to Schlatter (2003), the media warned Americans of the dangers of the extreme right during the 1960s (p. 38). The Minutemen were among the most extreme and thus got a large share of the publicity being given to the radical right at the time. Jones (1968) interviewed DePugh on many occasions. According to Finch (1983), "he [DePugh] was often available to the press" (p. 125). Evidently De-Pugh realized the potential the media had to help the Minutemen. Media attention could help recruit sympathetic persons who read newspaper accounts of the Minutemen into the organization. The media seemed fond of quoting DePugh. Indeed much of what DePugh said and wrote is worth quoting. However, the quotes often exaggerated the size and danger of the Minutemen. DePugh might claim he was misquoted. The media would surely claim that DePugh made the exaggerations himself. DePugh did have reason to exaggerate. It would have been beneficial for his enemies to believe the Minutemen organization was larger and more dangerous than it actually was.

Finch (1983) notes that DePugh used classified ads to promote the Minutemen and recruit members in the organization's early years (p. 117). According to Finch (1983) the Minutemen also told reporters about the Shiloh training session so they could come and report on the Minutemen (p. 117). The publicity seeking nature of the Minutemen no doubt helped them in the early years by making them known to the country. The Minutemen were extreme and extremism is interesting, even to moderates. Stories about the Minutemen training in military garb with sometimes illegal weapons made good newspaper stories. This publicity helped the Minutemen gain prominence in the early years but it most likely also helped bring them down in the later years. Many federal and state officials did not like the idea of a bunch of armed ultra-conservatives running around. The Minutemen constantly angered important people. This got them publicity but it also got them attention from law enforcement.

Chapter Nine

Crackdown on the Minutemen

The Minutemen had a flare for publicity. However, it was most often negative publicity. Very few, if any, newspaper articles ever ran stories praising the Minutemen. The reporters must not have believed DePugh and his fellow patriots, as he would call them, were brave men and women doing a noble thing. The Minutemen were not well liked by important people. Eventually law enforcement must have realized that the Minutemen were most likely committing crimes. They trained with firearms and explosives. Since firearms and explosive were, and are, highly regulated it would not have been easy to do everything the Minutemen did without breaking any laws. Federal and state law enforcement must have realized this and also realized they had the power to do significant damage to the Minutemen organization by convicting some of the more important members of the organization. This government strategy to get rid of the militant organization can best be termed the Crackdown on the Minutemen. All levels of law enforcement played a part in the crackdown but the FBI may have played the largest role. According to the FBI, there are approximately forty thousand pages of information concerning the Minutemen available from the Bureau through the Freedom of Information Act (L. Shaver, personal communication, January 10, 2007). This demonstrates the scope of the federal government's interest in the Minutemen organization. DePugh seems to have been the main target of government investigations. This is probably because he was the glue that kept the Minutemen organization together even during times of turmoil. As a result, DePugh had more run-ins with the law than any of the other Minutemen. Several of these incidents will be discussed in the following pages in addition to other major incidents involving suspected Minutemen.

DePugh's first run-in with the law that involved Minutemen activities began when he recruited two young women by the names of Linda and Patricia into the Minutemen in the summer of 1965 (Jones, 1968, p. 136). Janson (July 10, 1965) reports that the full names of the young women were Patricia Lucille Beal and Linda Frances Judd (p. 52). DePugh had recruited young women before. One was Cindy Melville whose mother complained to the authorities and attempted to get her out of the organization. Her mother claimed she was being held captive by the organization. However, no charges were ever brought against DePugh in that case, as Melville seemed to have been remaining in the organization of her own free will (p. 105-106). According to Jones (1968), DePugh's troubles began because Linda was only sixteen at the time of her recruitment into the organization and she had run away from home. DePugh claimed that he did not know how old she was when she joined the organization (p. 151). Patricia was twenty-one and divorced when she became involved in the organization (p. 137). According to Jones (1968), two versions have been offered concerning the events that

followed Linda and Patricia's recruitment into the Minutemen. Of course one version is from the girls themselves.
The other version is from DePugh and Cindy Melville (p.
137). Jones (1968) notes that the truth of the matter
probably lies somewhere in between the two stories, as it
often does (p. 137).

The girls' version will be summarized first. According to Jones (1968), Linda lived in an apartment in
Independence, Missouri, without paying any rent. One day
she met a man in the apartment complex who talked to her
about communism and told her she should join the
Minutemen. She decided to research the organization before making any decision. The young man later provided
her with some Minutemen literature and told her that if she
helped prepare it for mailing she wouldn't have to worry
about her rent. Around this time Patricia also met Robert
DePugh for the first time. Linda, who had just run away
from home, then came to stay with Patricia (pp. 137-138).
However, it is not known how Linda and Patricia first
became acquainted.

Jones (1968) goes on to note that according to the
girls, DePugh soon showed up at the apartment and
strongly suggested that the girls should join the Minutemen
but the girls refused. At five the next morning DePugh and
Cindy Melville supposedly forced their way into Patricia's
apartment and convinced the girls to go with them after
DePugh brandished a handgun. The girls went but objected
and after eating breakfast were driven to Richmond,
Missouri, about an hour away. Once at a house the girls
reportedly spent about two weeks under strict supervision
and were told to study Minutemen publications. Another
young female, Mary Tollerton, kept the girls company
during their stay. A visitor at the house during this time was
Walter 'Wally' Peyson, who was a prominent figure in
Minutemen activities. Among the subjects studied at the

house in Richmond were ways to use sex against the enemy. At some point the girls evidently realized they were being held captive. They eventually tried to leave the house but DePugh convinced them to return. They then were driven to Independence where they spent a couple days before escaping to Patricia's car, where they slept for the night. The next morning they were arrested by the Independence police, probably for the violation of a vagrancy ordinance. The girls then told their story to the Independence police and the FBI (pp. 138-141).

According to Jones (1968), the Independence police and FBI listened to the girls' story but were skeptical so they ordered a polygraph. According to the polygraph expert, the girls seemed to be mostly telling the truth. The FBI was also interested because the girls had told them they thought Wally Peyson had a machine gun. DePugh supposedly received word from a source within the Independence Police Department that trouble was brewing so a Minutemen training session was cancelled and several Minutemen who had been at the Independence training session fled but left their machine gun behind. The Jackson County prosecutor soon issued an arrest warrant for DePugh on a kidnapping charge. In the process of looking for DePugh several officers were allowed into a building at 613 East Alton in Independence. The building was still owned by DePugh at the time but a family of Minutemen by the name of Cannon occupied it. The officers looked around the building but failed to find DePugh. Among the items they did find were a land mine and a Thompson submachine gun. The automatic weapon was found in a furnace pipe in the basement. Supposedly, this gun had been left by California Minutemen who had fled the cancelled Independence training session. The submachine gun was confiscated that night [apparently the land mine was not] but it was later found to be deactivated (pp. 142-147).

According to Jones (1968) the search for DePugh then headed for his Norborne residence. The search party was joined by the Carroll County Sheriff's department and the Missouri Highway Patrol. The search party was met by three armed men. Troy Houghton, California leader of the Minutemen, was one of them. Wally Peyson and fifteen year-old John DePugh were the others. The three men allowed police to enter peacefully after being shown a warrant. Inside the house were Mary Tollerton and Dennis Mower, who were guarding Minutemen records which the search party did not have the authority to seize. Mower was the California Minuteman who supposedly left the sub-machine gun in Independence. Once again DePugh was not to be found (pp. 148-149).

Jones (1968) goes on to note that after the unsuccessful searches for DePugh, the FBI was ready to get involved. However, before they had a chance to look for DePugh themselves he surrendered, was arraigned, and posted bond. Shortly after DePugh posted bond the police got a search warrant for 613 East Alton to look for illegal weapons (p. 150) According to Jones (1968), in addition to a bazooka the following items were found in the building:

> Five cases of live dynamite, containing more than 200 sticks of explosives (although DePugh later was to boast they had overlooked two other cases); seven live hand grenades; five .45 caliber homemade but inoperable grease guns; a carbine; two "explosion (rocket) launchers"; a detonating device; a box of assorted Japanese land mines; one pound of TNT explosives; six rolls of detonating wire; seven boxes of wire fuse lighters; a timing device; two boxes containing seventy-five blasting caps; a "deac-

tivator"; a mousetrap booby-trap detonator; a .242 caliber Winchester automatic rifle; a role of detonating cable and one box of powder for explosives. (p. 151).

Jones (1968) also tells us how DePugh complained bitterly that many items were taken from the building that were not included on the inventory. DePugh refused to admit owning the weapons, although that would have given him the right to an accurate inventory (p. 151). Cindy Melville was arrested at 613 East Alton that night as a material witness but refused to answer any questions. She later posted bond and was released (p. 152).

The Minutemen's, or more specifically DePugh's, version of the alleged kidnapping, and the events leading up to the search of 613 East Alton is quite different than the girls' version. Jones (1968) notes that DePugh denied that Patricia's act of helping prepare Minutemen literature for the mail allowed her to pay less rent than she owed. DePugh claimed her apartment manager had never been a member of the Minutemen. In fact, DePugh claimed that Patricia was about to be evicted because she had been having parties at the apartment. DePugh and Cindy Melville concur that they went to Patricia's apartment about six in the morning but with no weapon. DePugh claimed that he never carried a concealed firearm. However, he would later be arrested with one in his car (p. 153). Jones (1968) goes on to note that DePugh claimed that after talking to the girls about the Minutemen, they voluntarily agreed to accompany DePugh and Melville to Richmond to undergo Minutemen training. DePugh said that they only remained in Richmond for one week and then were in Independence for the remainder of their stay with the Minutemen. DePugh also claimed the girls were free to leave at any time they wished and often went out in both Richmond and

Independence. According to DePugh, the girls never saw a machine gun belonging to Wally Peyson. DePugh said he took the girls back to Independence because they wanted to go, not because they had tried to escape the Richmond house. DePugh said the girls probably left 613 East Alton because he had become frustrated with their bad behavior and told them they needed to decide if they were really committed to the Minutemen. He also asserted that they most likely told the police their wild story because they were scared and wanted to get out of trouble with the law themselves. DePugh also accused the Independence police chief of being anti-Minutemen and the county prosecutor of being over ambitious. Both of these accusations were most likely true (pp. 154-157).

According to Jones (1968), DePugh claimed he did not know anything about the weapons and explosives that were seized at 613 East Alton. He claimed these things belonged to other Minutemen who had attended the Independence training session before it was cancelled (pp. 160-161). DePugh was finally indicted by a grand jury on charges of felony possession of bombs and contributing to the delinquency of a minor. DePugh was never indicted on the kidnapping charge. Both the possession of bombs and contributing charges were dropped over a year later (pp. 165-167).

George and Wilcox (1996) note that during the same time DePugh was under indictment for the 1966 incidents he was subpoenaed to bring forth the Minutemen's financial and membership records (p 227). DePugh adamantly refused to present the records and quite likely believed he would be jailed for contempt because of his refusal. However, he was never imprisoned. This may have been a partial result of assistance he received from the American Civil Liberties Union (ACLU). A U.S. Supreme Court ruling from 1958, *NAACP v. State of Alabama*, held that requiring the NAACP to give up its membership records to the state was a violation of the member's right to freedom of association. Ironically, it was decided that this case applied to the Minutemen as well (p. 227).

However, DePugh and the Minutemen would not have long to enjoy this small victory. According to George and Wilcox (1996), DePugh, Wally Peyson, and Troy Houghton were charged with conspiracy to violate the National Firearms Act in 1966. They were accused of "'transferring, making, receiving and possessing' automatic weapons and silencers" (p. 227). DePugh and Peyson were also charged with two additional counts of failing to pay a two hundred dollar tax required to possess a machine gun and machine pistol (pp. 227-228). An article in the *Kansas City Star* titled "U.S. Jury Indicts Minutemen Head" (August 21, 1966) described the arrest of DePugh in association with these charges. According to the article, DePugh was arrested by United States Marshals when his car was stopped on a Kansas City area interstate highway. Cindy Melville was with DePugh at the time of his arrest and attacked an Internal Revenue Service (IRS) agent after DePugh was placed in handcuffs. A barely legal sawed off shotgun and a pistol were found in the car but no attempt was made by DePugh or Melville to use the weapons. According to the article, five defendants were originally charged with conspiracy to violate the National Firearms Act. The two men originally charged in addition to those mentioned above were James Tollerton and John E. Blumer (pp. 1, 60). Charges against the other two men must have eventually been dropped.

According to George and Wilcox (1996), DePugh, Peyson, and Houghton were found guilty of all charges on January 17, 1967. Witnesses against the three men at trial were two former Minutemen, Jerry Brooks and undercover Bureau of Alcohol, Tobacco, and Firearms (BATF) agent

James Moore. Brooks later recanted his testimony but did so too late to do any of the defendants any good. DePugh was sentenced to four years in prison. Troy Houghton received a three year sentence and Wally Peyson received a two year sentence. Two counts were dismissed on appeal in this case and the third was remanded for a new trial (p. 228).

While under indictment for the charges mentioned above, DePugh also found himself in more hot water with the law. He was pulled over with a .38 caliber revolver in his car. He was charged with transporting a firearm across state lines while under a felony indictment. This was a violation of federal law under the National Firearms Act. Supposedly, DePugh transported the pistol from Des Moines to Kansas City and thus across state lines ("Minutemen Head Denies Guilt," October 8, 1966, p. 32). According to George and Wilcox (1996), DePugh received a one year sentence after being found guilty of this crime, which he eventually served in Leavenworth Penitentiary (pp. 228-229).

However, before DePugh and Wally Peyson could begin their sentences for the violations of the National Firearms Act they disappeared. According to George and Wilcox (1996), DePugh and Peyson were federal fugitives for a year and a half following their conviction (p. 228). According to Schlatter (2003), DePugh and Peyson ran to the small town of Truth or Consequences, New Mexico. There they rented a house under the aliases of "Ralph Cooper" for DePugh and "Jim" for Peyson (p. 37). According to Schlatter (2003), "DePugh was an avid outdoorsman and spent as much time as he could working on his survival skills in wilderness areas. He was attracted to New Mexico because it struck him as 'off the beaten path'—a place where he could disappear or pass unnoticed while furthering his rightist goals" (p. 37). The two men were well liked in the small New Mexico town and the locals were shocked when they heard that the two men were federal fugitives who were also supposedly connected with some bank robberies in the Pacific Northwest (p. 37). George and Wilcox (1996) note that DePugh explained his reason for fleeing while his convictions were being appealed was the excessive bonds being set by the court in his various cases (p. 228). DePugh explained his difficulties making bond to Finch (1983) as follows:

> When I went into hiding, I had—it was a really raw deal. I know everybody who serves time in prison tends to feel that way. But I was indicted on one charge after another—some of them totally without foundation, tentative hearsay evidence. But every time I was indicted I had to go to the bank, put up a bigger and bigger share of my company, money to make bond. When I finally went into hiding, I jumped bond on $480,000. That was money that went down the drain, and I never saw another dime of it. (p. 201).

According to Finch (1983), DePugh was finally to the point that he was unable to make bond when a thirty thousand dollar bond was set in Washington State for charges of conspiring to rob a bank. DePugh did not want to go to jail, and he did not feel that he deserved to go to jail, so he went into hiding (pp. 201-202).

Shortly before DePugh went into hiding he was charged with conspiracy to commit bank robbery in Washington. DePugh always claimed that had had no knowledge that bank robberies were going to occur. He claimed that he certainly did not have anything to do with planning the robberies himself. This was probably mostly true because the charge was eventually dropped. DePugh explained what he thought of the conspiracy charge to Finch (1983) as follows: "When the indictments came down on this Washington State bank robbery charge, it was as if two Catholics held up a filling station and they indicted the pope. That's how far removed I was" (p. 201). An article from the *New York Times* titled "Minutemen Founder Cited in Theft Plot" (March 5, 1968) explained that the FBI arrested seven men on January 26, 1968 for conspiracy to commit bank robberies. Neither DePugh nor Walter Peyson were among the seven men arrested in Washington on January 26. The men supposedly planned to rob four banks in the Seattle area. They reportedly planned to blow up bombs at a police station and a power plant as diversionary tactics for the bank robbery. However, the FBI arrested the conspirators before the bombs could be blown up and the banks robbed. DePugh denied that any of the men arrested in the plot were Minutemen. DePugh and Peyson were later indicted on conspiracy charges concerning the bank robbery plot and thirty thousand dollars bond was set for each man (p. 19).

Since DePugh and Peyson could not make bond they fled and the federal authorities began looking for them. According to George and Wilcox (1996), "For seventeen months DePugh and Peyson eluded the FBI, prompting a massive manhunt that consumed thousands of hours and hundreds of thousands of dollars" (p. 228). According to Schlatter (2003), DePugh and Peyson were eventually apprehended peacefully by federal and local law enforcement. They were arrested near U.S. highway 85 south of Truth or Consequences, New Mexico in July 1969 (p. 37). Jones (1969) notes that large quantities of weapons, explosives, and ammunition were found in the house the two men had rented [not at all unusual in raids of Minutemen residences] (pp. 375-376). DePugh was interviewed by reporters after his capture and claimed he and Peyson could have eluded the authorities permanently if they had concentrated on avoiding capture. However, they remained busy with Minutemen mailings and activities while in hiding which distracted their attention from avoiding capture. DePugh told reporters that the Minutemen had done well while he was underground and he had gotten a lot accomplished as national coordinator while in hiding. They stayed many different places while in hiding to avoid detection but they didn't stay anywhere long. They also used disguises to avoid being recognized. DePugh even reportedly used a hippie disguise ("DePugh Says He Eluded F.B.I. with Hippie Disguise", July 18, 1969, p. 11).

According to Jones (1969), DePugh and Peyson were returned to Kansas City after their capture. DePugh then began serving a one year sentence in Leavenworth Penitentiary for transporting a firearm across state lines while under a felony indictment, for which his appeals had failed. Peyson was unable to make bond and remained confined as well (p. 376). When Jones (1969) asked DePugh what would happen to the Minutemen now that he was confined DePugh replied "We'll keep going" (p. 376).

According to George and Wilcox (1996), DePugh received a four year prison sentence for his bond jumping incident. He claimed he was not guilty because he had not been notified of when to appear for trial, however, this claim did him little good (p. 229). DePugh made a statement to the court before he began his sentence. The statement was as follows:

> I stand before the court tried and found guilty. At this point it is no doubt traditional for the prisoner to offer some expression of repentance, but in all sincerity I cannot do so. To make matters worse, I cannot, in good conscience, give the court the slightest assurance that I will ever change my

ways....I would appreciate justice. But if I am not given justice, then I will accept injustice, and I will fashion even that into a weapon to continue the fight for principle, for pride, for honor. I will never give that up. (George & Wilcox, 1996, p. 229)

One good thing that can be said about Bob DePugh during his Minutemen years is that he was always a man of principle. He stood up for what he believed. He was willing to go to prison for what he believed. He sacrificed almost everything he had for the Minutemen cause. His financial losses were immense and family problems no doubt resulted from his Minutemen activities. His beliefs may have been unusual and his tactics were sometimes deplorable but he never gave up. When it would have been easier, and safer, to disband the Minutemen, DePugh kept on going. He believed the United States was in great danger and he was going to do something about it. He had his own ideology and he never did give that up.

DePugh was convicted and sentenced to ten years for violations of federal firearms statutes in 1970 ("Minutemen Chief Sentenced", October 10, 1970, p. 30). This was in addition to the previous charges for which some of his appeals had not been successful. According to George and Wilcox (1996), DePugh was sentenced in Albuquerque, New Mexico on October 10, 1970 (p. 229). They also note: "This time the prison gates slammed shut with a vengeance on Robert DePugh" (p. 229). DePugh must have thought he had become a political prisoner, and in some ways he probably was. George and Wilcox (1996) quote one of DePugh's writings: "From the past history of political prisoners, it is pretty obvious that the real reason the government wants to keep them confined is not because of their character but because of their political ideologies" (p. 229). If Robert DePugh had not attracted such great publicity and disfavor from government officials he probably would not have been sought after with such vigor. DePugh might have remained a free man.

According to Clarity (May 1, 1973), Robert DePugh was paroled after serving only four years. This was less than half of the maximum sentence he could have served. He was released from the federal penitentiary in Atlanta, Georgia [he was moved from Leavenworth to Atlanta at some point during his sentence] (p. 53). Clarity (May 1, 1973) goes on to note: "As he went free on parole, he said that although the Minutemen had been inactive during his imprisonment, they were still a force 'that an enemy would have to contend with'" (p. 53). DePugh also stated that he planned to talk with conservative leaders and that he would organize again if possible. The fifty year old DePugh then left for Norborne to return to work at Biolab (p. 53).

However, the leader of the now defunct Minutemen would find himself in more trouble with the law in 1991. According to Dine (September 14, 1991), Bob DePugh, sixty-eight, was arrested in Iowa and Des Moines police hauled out at least one thousand pictures of young females from his residence. DePugh was charged with sexual exploitation of a minor. The police had been tipped off by a film developing company in Sioux City, Iowa. Supposedly DePugh told the single mothers of the girls he photographed that their children were potential models. He would photograph them, gradually taking more provocative pictures. Many of the girls pictured were ten to thirteen years of age. The police found no evidence that DePugh was still involved with any paramilitary groups. However, he was often gone from his Iowa home for substantial periods of time and his cars still had Missouri license plates on them (p. 6-A).

According to Norton (September 14, 1991), Des Moines police stated: "At this point what we're seeing is child erotica, not child pornography" (p. A-1). However, police were still looking at the evidence. While the Des Moines investigation continued, the Carroll County Sheriff's Department served a search warrant for the house in Norborne, which DePugh still owned (p. A-1). Dauner (September 17, 1991) notes that the search of the Norborne house turned up more pictures of young girls, some nude. Carroll County Sheriff Willis Swearingin called the BATF in after finding weapons and explosives in the house (p. B-1). According to Dauner (September 17, 1991),

> Bureau agent Cynthia Grob seized five rifles, including one fully automatic rifle; a shotgun; five handguns, including one drilled for a silencer; and an 81mm British mortar. Army explosives experts destroyed one live mortar round, 250 pounds of unstable gunpowder, 104 rounds of 40mm high-explosive artillery rounds and 125 feet of fuse for explosives. Grob retained for evidence 19 practice rounds for the mortar. (p. B-1)

Thousands of rounds of ammunition, re-loading equipment, radio-controlled detonating equipment, and survival gear were also seized. DePugh was out on bond for the Iowa exploitation of minor charges at the time (p. B-1).

Dauner (September 18, 1991) notes that DePugh was arrested on a federal warrant and charged with being a felon in possession of a firearm on September 17, 1991. He was accused of constructive possession. He was ordered to be held without bond on that charge. He did not resist his arrest but instead cooperated with officers. The Carroll County Sheriff's Department also searched more buildings in Norborne and found more arms and evidence of a photographic dark room (p. C-3). Carroll and Dauner (September 20, 1991) note that Independence police believed DePugh had also photographed girls in that area and began a cooperative investigation with Des Moines police. However, photographs found by Independence police were not pornographic. All of the subjects in those photographs were clothed (p. C-1).

Dauner (September 27, 1991) notes concerning the reaction of Norborne citizens: "Norborne's annual Soybean Festival went off without a hitch last August. Now residents are learning they were lucky it didn't go out with a bang" (p. C-1). Federal agents discovered that the arms cache was very unstable, and that if it had detonated it could have leveled part of the small town. A fire in the building where the cache was stored could have caused a large explosion, injuring and killing many people. Norborne residents were not happy about the discovery (p. C-1). According to Dauner (September 27, 1991), "Margaret Brown, editor of the Norborne Democrat-Leader, said she was not amused when federal agents found the munitions. 'Why didn't they find that stuff back when they prosecuted him?' asked Brown" (p. C-1). Robert DePugh had once again made enemies out of the Norborne residents who did not think kindly of the idea of having a portion of their town blown up. Not much had been heard out of DePugh since he had last gotten out of prison, but his propensity for illegal arms collecting had once again caught up with him. Dauner (October 8, 1991) also notes that DePugh was eventually charged on three more counts of being a felon in possession of weapons or explosives. If convicted he was facing up to forty years in prison (p. B-1). According to Carroll (October 12, 1991), DePugh was also charged with three more counts of sexual exploitation of a minor in Des Moines, Iowa. Iowa authorities noted that they were not able to prosecute some cases because Iowa's sexual exploitation of a minor statute was not in effect before 1989 (p. C-8).

DePugh's defense to the illegal explosives charges was that the weapons were not his. Jackman (February 19, 1992) notes that William G. DePugh, Robert's brother, testified on his brother's behalf, saying that he moved several boxes to Norborne in 1970 but did not know what was in them. Robert was in prison in 1970 [perhaps the defense was trying to make the case that William had accidentally placed the weapons and explosives in Robert DePugh's house without his knowledge] (p. C-3). According to Jackman (February 21, 1992), "John DePugh said the guns in his mother's house were his, not his father's. His father, Robert DePugh, said he knew nothing about the guns" (p. C-1). Jackman (February 20, 1992) notes that DePugh also testified about the Minutemen and claimed that he had learned his lesson from his earlier illegal weapons convictions (p. C-1). However, the jury did not believe either John or Robert DePugh. Robert DePugh was convicted of three counts of possessing weapons illegally. He was acquitted on the fourth charge of possessing rocket propellant (p. C-1). According to Dauner (July 21, 1992), DePugh was sentenced to thirty months in prison for these convictions (p. B-1). Dauner (July 21, 1992) quoted DePugh as follows concerning his trial: "Denial of bail was equivalent to denial of a fair trial" (p. B-1). The prosecutor hoped for a harsher sentence for DePugh but failed to prove that DePugh had any involvement with paramilitary organizations since his first release from prison. DePugh was also ill at the time and his attorney claimed that he would not live long. The judge who sentenced DePugh received more than one hundred letters in support of him. All of this may have contributed to the relatively short prison sentence which was accompanied by a one thousand dollar fine (p. B-1). According to DePugh (October 20, 2006), he served the thirty month sentence in its entirety (See Appendix). DePugh (October 20, 2006) claims that he was only convicted two times in which he did not win on appeal (See Appendix). This was one of those times. There is no evidence that DePugh was ever convicted of the Iowa sexual exploitation of minors charges.

The Minutemen's legal troubles were certainly not limited to Robert DePugh and his close associates. Many members of the Minutemen found themselves in hot water throughout the 1960s and into the early 1970s. According to an article in the *New York Times* titled "U.N. Plot Traced by Ex-Minuteman" (November 10, 1966), Jerry Brooks, a former Minuteman turned government witness, testified that he had come up with an idea to put cyanide in the air-conditioning system at the United Nations. Brooks may have also been the source of an idea to assassinate Senator J.W. Fulbright, an Arkansas Democrat (p. 19). Jones (1968) interviewed Jerry Brooks and in that interview Brooks also indicated that the group thought about putting cyanide in the water system of the United Nations (p. 209). Whatever the plan was it was not carried out. Also, no one was ever charged with any crimes concerning the plot. However, Brooks may have turned government witness to avoid prosecution for his involvement in the U.N. conspiracy. Whatever the case, Brooks did become a government informer and witness. His testimony was obviously detrimental to DePugh and the Minutemen. DePugh (October 20, 2006) had his own thoughts concerning Jerry Brooks. "Jerry was a very unusual person. He had a truly photographic memory….But he was for sale and the F.B.I. had more money than I had. Jerry didn't want money but he had to live" (See Appendix). DePugh (October 20, 2006) seemed to believe that Brooks was only an informer because he had little choice. DePugh does not seem to hold this against Brooks today. The last DePugh knew of Brooks he had throat cancer and he does not know if Brooks is still living (See Appendix).

Minutemen were also involved in other criminal conspiracies. In New York State nineteen men were arrested on charges of conspiracy to commit arson with firebombs in 1966.

> Their prepared targets were said to have been three pacifist and leftist camps in New York State, Connecticut and New Jersey and the Brooklyn headquarters of Herbert Aptheker, a Marxist candidate for Congress. Tons of Firearms and ammunition were found in the defendants' possession. ("19 Minutemen Here", November 8, 1966, p. 47)

The men arrested were said to be ordinary men with everyday occupations ("Zero Hour", November 11, 1966, p. 52). It was certainly not unusual for Minutemen members to be seemingly ordinary working citizens. One hundred and ten law enforcement officers were involved in the raid to round up the nineteen men ("Sunday Patriots", November 11, 1966, p. 32). "Law enforcement officials charged that Minutemen disguised as hunters had planned to launch an attack against four separate targets" ("The Patriots", November 14, 1966, p. 31). Police allegedly confiscated one hundred and twenty five rifles, ten pipe bombs, five mortars, twelve machine guns, twenty-five hand guns, twenty brass knuckles, two hundred and twenty knives, a bazooka, three grenade launchers, six hand grenades, millions of rounds of ammunition, and a crossbow (p. 31). Information obtained from the FBI (October 31, 1966) contains a message which indicates that this inventory was highly inaccurate. The inventory obtained from the FBI is as follows:

> Forty-eight rifles, one bludgeon, six walkie talkies, five carbines, one brass knuckles, six machine guns, nine pistols, two mortars, three short wave radios, one truck equipped with short wave radio, one switch blade, five bombs, one bayonet, one shot gun, one rocket launcher, five thousand rounds of ammunition, one machete, two cross bows, five gallons inflammable liquid, one can gun powder and five camouflage suits. (p. 1).

Another message obtained from the FBI (November 16, 1966) indicates that Queens County District Attorney Nat Hentel made the original press release concerning the number of weapons seized and that this press release was greatly exaggerated (p. 1).

Jones (1968) notes that the Minutemen asked for members and sympathizers to contribute money to help the New York Minutemen (p. 312). It is not known whether or not DePugh had any knowledge of the conspiracy to attack the leftist camps. However, he was never charged with anything related to that incident. It is quite likely that he did not know about it and that the New York members were acting on their own, as individual Minutemen groups often did. Information obtained from the FBI (October 20, 1971) indicates that all charges against the New York Minutemen were eventually dismissed due to defective warrants and all men involved were freed (pp. 1-3).

Minutemen were also involved in another attempt to attack a pacifist camp in Voluntown, Connecticut (George & Wilcox, 1996, p. 233). This time the Minutemen came closer to succeeding but infiltrators in the organization still managed to tip off law enforcement in time to arrive while the attack was occurring. George and Wilcox (1996) quoted Nordon as follows:

This time the warning came too late….The
Minutemen opened fire and a brief gun battle
ensued before they threw down their weapons and
surrendered. Six people were shot in the melee—
one state trooper, four raiders and one of the
women residents, who was wounded in the hip
when a trooper's shotgun discharged as he side-
stepped a Minuteman's bayonet thrust (p. 234).

According to Jones (1969), the Connecticut camp was
called the Pacifist Farm and was run by the New England
Committee for non-violent action. It was one of the three
camps allegedly targeted in the earlier New York conspiracy. The Minutemen claimed the police came in firing
indiscriminately and the state trooper who was wounded
shot himself in the foot. The state police were quite sure he
was shot by a Minuteman. However, there is little doubt
that the female resident was shot accidentally by a state
trooper. All involved survived their wounds and five
Minutemen were arrested (pp. 356-358). All five Minutemen arrested in the case eventually plead guilty to
reduced charges. Three of the men involved received
sentences from two and one half to ten years in prison.
Another who had been blinded in the gun battle received
only one year. The man who was blinded had been shot
through both eyes, the bullet missing his brain by a fraction
of an inch. The fifth man received a one to nine year
sentence. The man who made his home available to plan
and carry out the attack from received probation. It is
possible that several other Minutemen were involved in the
raid but escaped during the gunfight (p. 359).

After the Connecticut incident there were no more
major incidents involving Minutemen with weapons.
However, Schlatter (2003) notes that Minutemen were
involved in the explosion of several devices across the

country intended to spread Minutemen leaflets. New York City; Houston, Texas; Kansas City, Missouri; Wichita, Kansas; Dallas, Texas; Carthage, Texas; Little Rock, Arkansas; and Washington D.C. were the locations where these devices were detonated. Some caused damage while others did not. The Washington D.C. explosion occurred near the White House. Some were successful in spreading their leaflets, others just made a loud noise (p. 48).

According to Schlatter (2003), ten college-aged men entered the administration building at the University of Chicago in February of 1969. They stormed in during a non-violent sit-in by left-wing protestors. A fist fight erupted between the Minutemen and the student protestors (p. 48). It is not known whether or not anyone was injured in this fist fight or if anyone was arrested. However, this was the last known incident in which Minutemen were involved in an altercation with leftists. After a few minor events in 1969 the Minutemen faded into obscurity. Little would be heard of them again.

Chapter 10

Conclusions

According to DePugh (October 20, 2006), the downfall of the Minutemen began after his first conviction for firearms violations. DePugh also notes that when the national and state organizations fell apart the only organizations left were at the band level. This was the end of the Minutemen because the bands did not do well without the higher-level organizations (See Appendix). However, DePugh (October 20, 2006) noted that there is still a group of Minutemen active in Virginia that had recently sent him some literature. However, DePugh did not claim to have any involvement with that group (See Appendix). Also, DePugh (October 20, 2006) commented that in a way today's border patrolling Minutemen of the American Southwest are related to DePugh's Minutemen. Some of them are former members of DePugh's Minutemen and they wrote him for an endorsement. However, he wanted no part of their organization (See Appendix). DePugh's Minutemen have been disbanded for many years now. It can be assumed that they were all but eliminated by the early 1970s, although small groups may have continued to live on. However, the Minutemen idea lives on today in other organizations, some of which consist of former Minutemen. In this way the Minutemen are not quite dead yet, although the national and state organizations have been for many years.

Today Bob DePugh lives in a mid-sized Missouri town not far from Norborne. DePugh (October 20, 2006) now considers himself disillusioned with politics. He notes: "I regret that I spent most of my lifetime in politics" (See Appendix). He does not believe that he has changed in his political ideology but instead the world's political ideologies have changed around him (See Appendix). Today DePugh suffers from Amyotrophic Lateral Sclerosis, commonly known as Lou Gehrig's disease. He has been told that he has less than a year to live and even now he is in considerable pain. However, he still has a lot he wants to accomplish. He would like to write any one of several books before he dies. DePugh stays busy even at his advanced age (See Appendix).

Bob DePugh is not your average man. This is evident by spending just a few minutes talking to him. He does not immediately strike you as a right-wing extremist. He does not jabber on with extremist rhetoric like so many leaders on the far right or far left do. He has a way of stating things which you can easily understand and see where he is coming from, even if you do not agree with him. He has the communication skills of a great leader. His writings are far more complex than would usually be expected of someone with his educational level. One usually either emphatically agrees with his ideas or thinks they are the craziest things one has ever heard. Indeed, it is sometimes hard to decide whether Bob DePugh is a genius or a screwball. It is not hard to believe that DePugh's goal of saving the United States from Communism was noble. However, his tactics for doing so were often deplorable.

There seems little doubt that the Minutemen had the potential to be a dangerous organization. They were violence prone and their leadership was often unable to exercise much control over individual members. As a result of this danger it is probably for the best that the Minutemen faded into obscurity before any of their acts caused any great harm. However, the Minutemen had nobody to blame but themselves for their failure. They attracted bad publicity and angered government officials in a way that few other organizations have been able to. They turned the majority of Americans against them because of their extremist tactics. The Minutemen were victims of their own extremism. Extremism that they believed was in the defense of liberty, but extremism none the less. Had the Minutemen taken a more moderate approach they probably could have existed in relative peace without much government interference. However, they did not believe the nation could be saved with the moderate approach. In that way the Minutemen were victims of their own beliefs.

Had "The Day" come in which the United States was invaded by Communists, the Minutemen might have been thought of in a much different way. They might have played a part in saving the liberties we today take for granted as Americans from the oppression of communism. However, the Minutemen's fatal flaw, apart from their extremist tactics, was their overestimation of the probability of Communist invasion. There is no doubt that communism was dangerous, especially during the time of the Minutemen, but the Communist invasion never came.

If one were to ask Robert DePugh if the United States was still in great danger today he would probably reply that it is. However, he would not say that communism is the danger today. He would probably explain other dangers Americans face today, which are perhaps even more serious than communism was in the 1960s. As a result there is still fertile ground for organizations like the Minutemen. They may claim to be fighting a different foe but they always believe they are saving America from something. They always consider themselves patriots just as the Minutemen did.

Finally, it is prudent to take a look at the effects of the Minutemen. On the Radical Right their effect may have been felt the greatest. They did their own part to give conservative extremists the violent reputation they have today. They probably also helped cause the passage of various laws banning paramilitary organizations. The Minutemen hurt the radical right in a way but they also proved radical right-wing organizations were not by necessity white supremacist organizations. Also, many of the Minutemen's ideas live on, some in the radical right, others in libertarian organizations.

The Minutemen probably had little effect on communism. They never got their chance to fight Communists. They never exposed many Communist subversives either. If anything the Minutemen may have strengthened communism during the 1960s by taking attention away from it and focusing it on themselves.

The Minutemen had a great effect on some of their own members. Many former Minutemen probably wished they never joined the organization because of the trouble it caused them. The members who served prison time were probably hurt the most. Of those, Bob DePugh has probably suffered the worst. Not only did he spend time in prison, but his wife eventually divorced him, probably partially because of his devotion to the Minutemen cause. He also suffered the stigma associated with his Minutemen activities. It is also certain that he could have been much better off financially, and otherwise, if he had never been national coordinator of the Minutemen.

The Minutemen probably had little effect on society. Most people would probably not know who the Minutemen were if they were brought up in conversation. Those that do know of them probably have little idea what the organization was, other than a group of gun carrying extremeists. However, it is possible that some Minutemen ideas have had an effect on some modern radical organizations and thus on society, but this is impossible to prove.

The Minutemen flourished only briefly in history, and they may have made little impact, but their story is worth telling not just because it is intriguing but because history often repeats itself. It would be little surprise if a group much like the Minutemen emerged in the future to fight some threat similar to communism. If so it would be wise to understand Robert DePugh's Minutemen and what they were as well as what they were not. Today the Minutemen are mostly forgotten, but perhaps we should remember them. They should not be judged based solely on their extremism. They may teach us some valuable lesson yet.

Perhaps this lesson might be that we should be ever vigilant of a powerful government. Just as the founding fathers recognized an oppressive government and fought to free themselves from it, the time may come again when this is necessary. Although the Minutemen may have misjudged when that time would come, they recognized that no government of man is immune from tyranny. We might do well to remember this because no person can know what the future may hold in store.

References

19 Minutemen here linked to DePugh. (1966, November 8). *The New York Times*, p. 47.

Carroll, D., & Dauner, J.T. (1991, September 20). Snapshots taken at area inn: Man who faces sex charge photographed girls in Independence. *The Kansas City Star*, p. C1.

Carroll, D. (1991, October 12). DePugh faces more charges: Former leader of an ultraright group named in pornography case. *The Kansas City Star*, p. C8.

Carroll, M. (1966, October 31). Minutemen idea grew out of duck hunt in 1959. *The New York Times*, p. 40.

Clarity, J.F. (1973, May 1). DePugh of Minutemen paroled. *The New York Times*, p. 53.

Coast ban sought on rightist militia. (1964, January 7). *The New York Times*, p. 39.

Dauner, J.T. (1991, September 17). Munitions discovered in residence of rightist accused of sex charge. *The Kansas City Star*, p. B1.

Dauner, J.T. (1991, September 18). DePugh arrested on firearms charge: Ex-Minutemen leader already is subject of child pornography inquiry. *The Kansas City Star*, p. C3.

Dauner, J.T. (1991, September 27). Arms cache was unstable, officials say DePugh's Stockpile made Norborne, Mo., a potential time bomb. *The Kansas City Star*, p. C1.

Dauner, J.T. (1991, October 8). Grand jury indicts ex-leader of ultraright group. *The Kansas City Star*, p. B1.

Dauner, J.T. (1992, July 21). DePugh sentenced to 30 months in prison. *The Kansas City Star*, p. B1.

DePugh, R.B. (n.d.). *What's wrong with communism?* Minutemen pamphlet, pp. 1, 4, 9-10.

DePugh, R.B. (1970). *Blueprint for victory* (3rd ed.). Norborne, MO: DePugh.

DePugh, R.B. (1973). *Can you survive?: Guidelines for resistance to tyranny for you and your family*. El Dorado, AZ: Desert.

DePugh, R.B. (1974). *Beyond the iron mask*. Norborne, MO: Salon.

DePugh quitting Minutemen post: Says right-wing group will operate in secrecy. (1967, January 24). *The New York Times*, p. 34.

DePugh rejoins Minutemen citing internal dissension. (1967, May 2). *The New York Times*, p. 40.

Dine, P. (1991, September 14). Ex-survivalist held in child sex case. *St. Louis Post-Dispatch*, p. 6A.

Epstein, B.R., & Forster, A. (1967). *The radical right: Report on the John Birch Society and its allies.* New York: Random House.

Farber, D., & Roche, J. (Eds.). (2003). *The conservative sixties.* New York: Peter Lang.

Federal Bureau of Investigation. (1966, October 31). Bureau teletype concerning the Minutemen. Obtained under the Freedom of Information Act January 19, 2007, p. 1.

Federal Bureau of Investigation. (1966, November 3). Report on the Minutemen. Obtained under the Freedom of Information Act January 19, 2007, p. 5.

Federal Bureau of Investigation. (1966, November 16). Airtel concerning the Minutemen. Obtained under the Freedom of Information Act January 19, 2007, p. 1.

Federal Bureau of Investigation. (1967, April 21). Report on the Minutemen. Obtained under the Freedom of Information Act January 19, 2007, pp. 15a-15e.

Federal Bureau of Investigation. (1968, February 8). Report on the Minutemen. Obtained under the Freedom of Information Act January 19, 2007, p. 3.

Federal Bureau of Investigation. (1968, July 31). Report on the Minutemen. Obtained under the Freedom of Information Act January 19, 2007, pp. 16a-16d, 29.

Federal Bureau of Investigation. (1969, November 4). Report on the Minutemen. Obtained under the Freedom of Information Act January 19, 2007, pp. 14, 18-20.

Federal Bureau of Investigation. (1971, October 20). Report on the Minutemen. Obtained under the Freedom of Information Act January 19, 2007, pp. 1-3.

Finch, P. (1983). *God, guts, and guns: A close look at the radical right*. New York: Seaview/Putnam.

George, J., & Wilcox, L. (1996). *American extremists: militias, supremacists, Klansmen, Communists, & others*. Amherst, NY: Prometheus.

Harry, A., & Overstreet, B. (1964). *The strange tactics of extremism*. New York: W.W. Norton.

Hill, G. (1961, November 12). Minutemen guerrilla unit found to be small and loosely knit. *The New York Times*, pp. 1, 76.

Isserman, M., & Kazin, M. (2000). *America divided: The civil war of the 1960s*. New York: Oxford University.

Jackman, T. (1992, February 19). Founder of ultrarightist group goes on trial over weapons cache: Photos of teen-agers led officers to his house. *The Kansas City Star*, p. C3.

Jackman, T. (1992, February 20). Defendant's son takes blame for arms cache: Minutemen founder didn't put weapons in buildings, son testifies. *The Kansas City Star*, p. C1.

Jackman, T. (1992, February 21). DePugh convicted on gun charges: Jury not swayed by testimony of son that the weapons were his. *The Kansas City Star*, p. C1.

Janson, D. (1961, November 13). Chief Minuteman upsets his town. *The New York Times*, p. 23.

Janson, D. (1965, July 10). Minutemen chief surrenders, accused of kidnapping 2 girls. *The New York Times*, p. 52.

Janson, D. (1969, July 18). DePugh says he eluded F.B.I. with hippie disguise. *The New York Times*, p. 11.

Jones, Jr., J.H. (1968). *The Minutemen*. Garden City, NY: Doubleday.

Jones, Jr., J.H. (1969). *A private army* (Revised ed. of *The Minutemen*). Toronto, Ontario: Collier-Macmillan.

Kennedy, J.F. (1961, January 29). *Roosevelt Day commemoration message*. Retrieved January 18, 2007, from http://www.jfklibrary.org/Historical+Resources/Ar chives/Reference+Desk/Roosevelt+Day+Comme moration+Message.htm

Levitas, D. (2002). *The terrorist next door: The militia movement and the radical right*. New York: St. Martin's Griffin.

Mallett, W.E. (1965). *The Reuther Memorandum: Its applications and implications*. Washington, D.C.: Liberty Lobby.

Microsoft. (2002). Communism. *Microsoft Encarta Encyclopedia*, para. 2,3.

Minutemen chief sentenced to 10 years on arms counts. (1970, October 10). *The New York Times*, p. 30.

Minutemen cleared of anti-U.S. actions. (1964, February 4). *The New York Times*, p. 27.

Minutemen founder cited in theft plot. (1968, March 5). *The New York Times*, p. 19.

Minutemen head denies guilt in firearms case. (1966, October 8). *The New York Times*, p. 32.

Minutemen's soft-sell leader: Robert B. DePugh. (1961, November 12). *The New York Times*, p. 76.

Norton, B. (1991, September 14). Head of rightist army charged in sex case. *The Kansas City Star*, p. A1.

On Target. (1966, January 1). Norborne, MO: Minutemen, pp. 1, 8.

The patriots. (1966, November 14). *Newsweek, 68*, 31.

Posner, G. (1993). *Case closed: Lee Harvey Oswald and the assassination of JFK*. New York: Anchor.

Schlatter, E.A. (2003). Extremism in the defense of liberty: The Minutemen and the radical right. In D. Farber & J. Roche (Eds.), *The conservative sixties* (pp. 37- 50). New York: Peter Lang.

Senator Young asks curb on Minutemen. (1965, February 5). *The New York Times*, p. 15.

Sunday patriots. (1966, November 11). *Time Magazine, 88,* 32.

U.N. plot traced by ex-Minuteman. (1966, November 10). *The New York Times*, p. 19.

U.S. jury indicts Minutemen head: DePugh arrested on charge of illegal firearms. (1966, August 21). *The New York Times*, p. 1, 60.

Zero hour for the Minutemen. (1966, November 11). *Life, 61,* 52.

Interview with Robert DePugh
October 20, 2006

<u>Side A</u>

Eric Beckemeier: So could you tell me about how the Minutemen idea started?

Robert DePugh: Well it started in Independence, Missouri at a little coffee shop on Lexington Street a half a block west of the square.

Eric Beckemeier: Was it purely your idea or were there other people involved in the beginning of the Minutemen?

Robert DePugh: Well there were quite a few people that sort of got in the habit of meeting, you know, for a cup of coffee along in the morning there, you know. One was a veterinarian who had his office on Lexington Street but it was some distance away and you know there was also an insurance agent. Let me just say, you know, pretty typical small town business. It wasn't like you know.

Eric Beckemeier: Pretty normal people who got involved at the beginning.

Robert DePugh: You know we talked about everything, not just politics you know. I'm trying to think of the time frame because there was no date that you could just say this started.

Eric Beckemeier: I know I've read like 1958.

Robert DePugh: It was probably the late 50's, '55 to '60, you know, we had this conversation. In those days of course we all thought that communism was a bad thing and we all thought that our government was an anticommunist government. And then in the course of human events this was gonna come into a conflict you know as the Bay of Pigs didn't happen but it was, you know, it was something that I think a lot of people realized. You know that we were gonna have some kind of a conflict. So sort of just gradually the idea crept into the conversation that we were well aware that that, you know, there was a talk radio show in Kansas City at the time and, uh, we were talking about Castro being up in the mountains fighting a guerilla warfare against Batista and the idea sort of evolved well you know if the Communists ever do invade this country we should reverse the situation on them and we should be prepared to fight a guerilla war, you know, if our military forces became neutralized by the threat of an atomic war, you know, so that the conventional forces were the only war that was going to be fought, you know, we envisioned that the mutually assured destruction would prevail and since there would be no atomic war, you know, eventually perhaps the overwhelming might of the Soviet Union and their billions of people in China and Russia combined. But we were also thinking that well we would be totally unprepared to fight such a war, and a guerilla war, so well we thought the thing to do is start preparing in advance so we started stockpiling for our own survival situation and that's probably where we made a mistake, you know, because first of all we did not conceive of the fact that our own government had already been infiltrated to this degree. We could not conceive that our government would think we were doing anything bad. I had other friends who were gun fanciers. And you know after the Bay of Pigs invasion we began to supply some of the anti-Castro groups with guns, you know. Probably the worst thing I ever did was to ride in a pickup truck taking a whole load of guns that we had traveled around the United States, this other fella and I, asking all our gun dealer friends "Would you volunteer?" You know with what he had we could take down to Alpha 66. Low and behold, you know, it was sort of amazing to us. I was a licensed firearms dealer. I had my federal permit. One of my friends had a manufacturers permit to manufacture machine guns and silencers so we thought what the hell is the government complaining about, you know, but eventually it got harder and harder and we began to realize in our own mind at least, you know, probably there would be some people that still would debate but we came to the conclusion that hell our own government has already gone Communist. They don't want us to defend individual freedom, the Second Amendment means nothing at all to them, the right to keep and bear arms is a façade. But it took us a long, long time to wake up to that fact or that presumption as we saw it. But I think McNamara was the secretary of defense at that time and from our contacts with Alpha 66, which was the Cuban underground, we knew about the missiles being unloaded in Cuba long before the American public did and it was Senator Church I think from Idaho that we contacted by mail and told him what was going on. These missiles were being unloaded in Cuba and finally, you know, he made a statement in Senate to, you know, have enough surveillance and finally it was McNamara or someone who got on TV and told about how we had decided there are missiles being unloaded and in Cuba, you know. A phony, phony façade. And then they told about the missile silos were being destroyed in Cuba and I remember watching him on television showing these pictures of these earth works being moved and he said, you know, "The earth is being churned by bulldozers as these missile silos are being destroyed." I don't know, I think there was some sort of threat and counter threat. We had put our own missiles in Turkey by that time and so but anyhow I'm trying to think here, I'm trying to recount a little bit from your point of view what the thinking was. The conversation of all the people that met from time to time in the coffee shop. There were a couple duck hunters in the group. Some of us were planning to go duck hunting. I think up at Swan Lake. So with this frame of mind somebody said well, you know, if worst comes to worst we'll just form our own guerilla organization and so there was never really ever any one time that I really started the organization myself. I sort of evolved into it as other people dropped out, you know, and finally there were, you know, basically a few people, about ten. I would say that not all of them were from Independence but most of them from Independence that, uh, formulated this idea and finally decided let's do it, you know. I was setting while I was in the process of moving my business up to Norborne, and I was setting in the café up there one time reading a talk that had been given by John Kennedy and I think he was a Congressman at the time. He was not President yet and he said, well, "We need a nation of Minutemen." That was in his talk and I thought, well, we were kind of thinking, well, "Did we even need a name for the organization?" and if we did we were anticipating that the left wing propaganda would find fault with any name we came up with and we thought, "Well that's a good two hundred year old concept and surely they can't find any fault in that," so with John Kennedy's help that's where the name evolved. Why he was killed? I don't pretend to know but, uh, there were quite a few of us that thought he really betrayed the nation, you know. There was supposed to be Air Force support which never developed. Some of the people that were in on the Bay of Pigs invasion were friends of mine and one man I think worked for me a while and we used to listen to this talk radio thing, you know, so he went down and he joined with the people at Alpha 66, you know at one point would eventually become Alpha 66.

Eric Beckemeier: Yeah.

Robert DePugh: At that time there was no such name but, uh, he was captured and the thing of it was that these guys that went in on this invasion were not allowed to put any ammunition in their guns until they hit the beach. When they did they found out that the ammunition that had been in these cases would not fit the guns they had, you know. They had .30 caliber guns and 9 millimeter ammunition and so we figured the whole thing was meant to fail to begin with and after that we weren't really sure about, uh, Kennedy, you know J.F.K. Was he the instigator of the rebel cause or was he a victim, you know? And when he was assassinated, you know, and later on after Bobby was killed we concluded that J.F.K had to be the victim. He's not the, uh, but over the years that the Minutemen organization existed and there is still a remnant.

Eric Beckemeier: Yeah.

Robert DePugh: Uh, well let's see. I'll probably run on to it sometime before your paper is due and but I received some literature, you know, in the mail two or three weeks ago from a group in Virginia that is still active and reprinted a copy of what they call the *Minutemen Handbook*. There was never such a handbook, you know, but this is one of the problems that the quote right-wing has always had. The fact is that there has always been fake organizations that claim to be this or claim to be that. For example, I don't particularly consider the Klan as being part of the right-wing but the one part of the Klan that used to fairly legitimate I would say, and by legitimate I mean they were doing what they said they were doing, was Bob Shelton's group the United Klans of America. Well along came, uh, more and more quote Klan groups that claimed to be Klan groups but were totally out for the money, you know, they were mercenaries and, you know. Once again I would say that George Lincoln Rockwell's group, you know, the American Nazi Party was a phony organization, totally phony you know. It was mercenary and, uh, but even that group had a half a dozen imitators that were even more phony than he was. It was a matter of who could steal from the thieves. Uh, so looking back on the Minutemen organization it was uh a hopeless effort (inaudible) but I feel that the German saying "Too soon old and too late smart" applies and, uh, of that the people themselves that are still remnants of the Minutemen organization are, you know, uh gullible. The American people in my estimation are the most gullible people, you know, as a nation. If I went to jail it was not because I was a criminal, it was because I was stupid.

Eric Beckemeier: Yeah.

Robert DePugh: So that is the general outline. What you've got on your tape now.

Eric Beckemeier: Yeah.

Robert DePugh: And anything else basically is filling in the details to give you enough material to do the paper.

Eric Beckemeier: OK. Were the Minutemen organized into small bands, loosely organized bands?

Robert DePugh: Yeah, the closest we came to having a national organization was the fact that we had state directors. Each state had some one person who was sort of the leader of that state.

Eric Beckemeier: And do you think that the being loosely organized, did that lead to infiltration by your enemies or by the government?

Robert DePugh: By being loosely organized, I think, the fact that we were loosely organized is the only reason we survived as long as we did. The infiltration would have come either way.

Eric Beckemeier: OK. Did the Minutemen have like a military style rank?

Robert DePugh: No. No, basically beneath the state level it was mostly a matter of people thought this idea up by themselves or maybe they heard, read something in the newspapers about it, uh, and then wrote in and said "How can I join?" We would put them in touch with the people in that state, the coordinator or someone in that area but we never did encourage them to self identify themselves.

Eric Beckemeier: Did you use like numbers for identification?

Robert DePugh: Yeah.

Eric Beckemeier: OK. So like how many members were there in the beginning and how did the membership numbers fluctuate through the years?

Robert DePugh: It was hard say where the membership started and where it ended, you know, because oftentimes the word quote organization unquote was so loose that to define the number of members or to say where the membership left off and the fellow travelers, the sympathizers, began and there was really no dues and see, uh, state coordinators sort of financed our own area and collected, you know, the contributions. Most of the state coordinators were people who were fairly well fixed financially. They were professional people for the most part or they were business people because it was as far as the Minutemen were concerned, there was no profit made by anybody, you know. If I hadn't had a fairly good business I couldn't have done what I did. If the director of the New York hadn't had a very good job working for a big company that happened to be a pharmaceutical company he couldn't have done what he did.

Eric Beckemeier: Uh, were memberships sometimes revoked? Would the Minutemen sometimes revoke somebody's membership, you know, kick them out of the organization?

Robert DePugh: Yeah we did but it was rare. It was rare for two reasons. One, when you kick somebody out then you turn the claimed friend into a devout enemy.

Eric Beckemeier: Yeah. Were there any female Minutemen?

Robert DePugh: Yes, many. I would say that twenty percent were.

Eric Beckemeier: So do you think that financing the Minutemen through Biolab kind of, do you think that hurt your business in the end?

Robert DePugh: It ruined it, you know. I won't say it ruined it, you know, because Biolab never went completely bankrupt, you know, but I could've been a millionaire several times over if I'd of just stuck to business.

Eric Beckemeier: Yeah. So you certainly weren't in it for the money then, because I know there is a lot of speculation that you were making money off the Minutemen somehow.

Robert DePugh: Whenever anybody says that ask them "How?" you know. They don't understand the situation.

Eric Beckemeier: So how many states had Minutemen working in them?

Robert DePugh: Every state. All the continuous 48 and then there were at least sympathetic organizations overseas as well.

Eric Beckemeier: OK.

Robert DePugh: The, uh, its sort of strange the way the political situation has evolved. Some of the people who I would've once considered our worst enemies are now friends, you know. George Orwell's book *1984* was almost prophetic. One of the things, you know, that they spoke of in *1984* the book was the newspeak. Uh, and the fact that as Big Brother exerted his control, you know, and the dictatorship began to fall apart, uh, things in the newspeak, in the required speak, uh, no one was supposed to say anything bad. Everything was supposed to be wonderful but it got to the place where things could no longer be, business could no longer be conducted with everything being rosy. So they had to change the law a little bit to the point that if the opposite, if you wanted to say things were good you couldn't say things were good you had say things were un-bad. You know anything could be considered just the opposite by putting *un* in front of it. And of course from my point of view now that is what has happened in the United States, you know. I had a, a, uh, (inaudible) many years ago I was talking on the phone to and she happened to be one of the female members from long ago and she said, "Well I used to be a conservative and now I'm liberal." And I said "well are you sure you have changed or has it just been terminology that has changed?" And I think that today a great many people who were the sort of very (inaudible) type of conservative, uh, would almost be considered liberals today. The idea that there is a religious right in this country is pure bologna. You know you don't have a religious right in this country, you've got a bunch of born again brain dead people. I say that just to sort of let you know. (Inaudible)

Eric Beckemeier: You know if today if you had to identify yourself as having a certain political viewpoint what would you consider yourself to be?

Robert DePugh: Disillusioned. I am absolutely disillusioned as far as politics are concerned I regret that I wasted most of my lifetime in politics.

Eric Beckemeier: Kind of speaking of politics, could you tell me a little bit about the Patriot Party?

Robert DePugh: Well that was formed I guess, in what? 1950-1955 [DePugh probably meant 1960-1965] somewhere along in there because we were beginning to wake up to the fact that guerrilla warfare was an illusion, a mirage. That if we cannot do it politically we're not going to be able to do it any way. So we tried to form the Patriotic Party and at about the same time other people were forming the American Party. And that's where the collectivists had it over us, you know. Basically, what we thought of ourselves, not as right-wing or left-wing, but as individualists, you know. The organization was the individualists versus the collectivists and the collectivists may have been right in that because of their collectivism they could always get it together. The individualists because of our philosophy of individualism were never able to get it together. We always fought among ourselves. It was competition and basically if you talk about the quote religious right in the formation of the Patriotic Party, that is when the religion became a dominate issue. The Minutemen would almost be an organization of agnostics. But the quote Christians, for lack of a better word, became the majority within the change to the Patriot Party and so there are still quite a few of those groups existing under different names. And we sort of make the pretext of being friendly but its becoming more and more difficult. Are you surprised?

Eric Beckemeier: No. So did the party endorse any certain candidates or run any candidates for elections?

Robert DePugh: Yeah, when it came down to the, I think the second national meeting, we endorsed George Wallace and I would say that was not because the majority of the organization thought George Wallace was a great guy. It was because that was the matter of (inaudible) you could say, you know. We needed a candidate that was not a Democrat or a Republican and we thought George Wallace was our man.

Eric Beckemeier: Yeah. So do you think the assassination attempt on him, do you have any thoughts on that?

Robert DePugh: I think the guy that tried to kill him was a kook.

Eric Beckemeier: You don't think it was political?

Robert DePugh: No. He may have had his own political philosophy but I don't think you could say it was in any event racial in any way. Things racial or not political. There is a distinction.

Eric Beckemeier: There's been some speculation in a few books that I've read about the Minutemen. That they seemed to consider the Minutemen to be, like, almost, a white supremacist organization. Was it that way or was that the intent at a time?

Robert DePugh: That was never the intent from the organization's point of view. We had several quote black members and we had some Jewish members but when they joined either the state coordinator or someone else basically always said "OK, so you're welcome but we want to tell you ahead of time, within a certain area you're welcome but, you know, its basically going to be a one way street. If you want to be a member of the organization we're going to look to you to give us information. We're not going to give you information. If you want to join on that basis its fine." I had a member in Vermont who came down to visit me. He was not only an African American, he was a dark complected African American. He was a very dark complected African American and he said "Bob the only time, you know, I was adopted by a white man and lady in Vermont and until I went to college the only Negro I ever saw was when I looked in the mirror." And he was a valuable kind of member because he was able to infiltrate all kinds of organizations.

Side B

Eric Beckemeier: It should be going again. OK.

Robert DePugh: It was the same way with the Jewish members. We had surprisingly. I think it would be surpriseing to most people to realize how many we had. Not all of them admitted to being Jewish but there was, you know, I can't remember his name right now but there was one fellow who was really in his mind an anti-Jew himself but he was racially a Jew.

Eric Beckemeier: Yeah.

Robert DePugh: Be he was not religiously.

Eric Beckemeier: There are a few names that in my research have kept coming up and I just wondered if you could tell me a little bit about some of these people and how they were involved in the Minutemen: Kenneth Goth, Walter Peyson, and Jerry Brooks.

Robert DePugh: Well Kenneth Goth, when he was in college became a member of the Communist Party and when the time came that Hitler and Stalin formed what they called the Hitler-Stalin pact, you know, then he became totally disillusioned with communism and became a, uh, staunch anti-Communist. He just flipped and formed an organization he called the Soldiers of the Cross. And he became a Baptist minister and I was a little bit skeptical of him at one time when I first heard about him, you know, but I think he was as good a patriot as this country ever had. When he flipped he flipped all the way and he was not, despite being a Baptist minister and having this quote church camp and so forth, he was at one time I heard him say "Well Bob the problem with most Christians is they become so heavenly minded that they're of no earthly value," so Ken was always of earthly value.

Eric Beckemeier: How about Walter Peyson?

Robert DePugh: Well Wally is still my friend and he comes to visit me ever so often.

Eric Beckemeier: How about Jerry Brooks?

Robert DePugh: Jerry was a very unusual person. He had a truly photographic memory. You know I, uh, had always heard of him and I knew him well enough to know Jerry was, he could recite data information, you know, endlessly. And he and I were setting in a café up on Grand Avenue in Kansas City one day and I said "Jerry I've heard this about you and I've seen you repeat things seemingly from memory. Telephone numbers of people's houses that you went into and uh saw the phone number on their phone and seemed to remember it months later." So he said well, you know, and we were just setting there and he was kind of in a way kooky acting, you know, a little excitable. And he said let's get out of here, you know. So we went I think this was about the corner of 8th or 9th and Grand and we walked two or three blocks up toward the federal building. We crossed the street and walked back and went back to the same coffee shop and he reached over and took a stack of paper napkins with a ball point pen and started writing down license numbers, and then we walked back up the same route and checked the license numbers and, except for a few that were then obviously moved, he remembered every damn one of those license numbers and he was when we were walking up, you know, he was talking, you know, and he would. It was not at all obvious that he even glanced at these license numbers. So he had a tremendous talent.

Eric Beckemeier: Yeah.

Robert DePugh: And for that reason, you know, he would make tape recordings of information and mail it to me or write it to me that was almost unbelievable so he was a valuable source of information. But he was for sale.

Eric Beckemeier: Yeah.

Robert DePugh: And the F.B.I. had more money than I had. Jerry didn't want money but he had to live, you know. So when he got hard up he went to the F.B.I. and sold them information. But I've heard, the last time I knew anything of him that he had cancer of the throat so I don't even know if he's still alive or not but if Jerry walked in right now I'd say, "Hey Jerry have a cup of coffee," you know.

Eric Beckemeier: Yeah.

Robert DePugh: I could never get mad at Jerry.

Eric Beckemeier: So let's see. Where did you go to school and what educational level did you achieve.

Robert DePugh: Well the educational level is easy. I don't have any degrees. I went to University of Missouri for a year and a half before the War. I went to the University of Colorado about a year during the war and Kansas State two and a half years. Washburn University half a year. And I took some correspondence courses with Georgia Tech. So, and I've learned more in the last year than I have in the previous 70 years. Everything I learned in my field, biochemistry you know, everything I learned has either been proven wrong or is out of date. I won't say everything. The periodic table is still a thing.

Eric Beckemeier: But they're trying to add to that.

Robert DePugh: They keep adding to it and there is still another one they've added to just in the last week or two.

Eric Beckemeier: There are a lot of rumors around Norborne still today that you, or the Minutemen, or some combination dug tunnels under Norborne. Were there any tunnels?

Robert DePugh: Nah.

Eric Beckemeier: I know that the most common one that I've heard is that there was a tunnel underneath the old Biolab building that went out underneath the railroad tracks and came up in between them. That's the most common one I've heard.

Robert DePugh: No, there were not tunnels anywhere. Not even one feet.

Eric Beckemeier: Did you ever, were there ever any plans to do anything like that?

Robert DePugh: No.

Eric Beckemeier: How about any bomb shelters?

Robert DePugh: Well back in the day when my brother Bill worked for me at Biolab, you know, and bomb shelters were quote the fad we thought we would start digging a bomb shelter in the basement of Biolab and, uh, one time he and I were at a grocery store in Independence and they had a sale on cheese and we thought well we needed some survival food in the bomb shelter. So we bought fifty pounds of cheese. We had fifty one pound sticks but the cheese was all eaten before the bomb shelter got finished and we thought well why go any further so, you know, we had done some talking but that was it.

Eric Beckemeier: So other than the bomb shelter that you were talking about did the Minutemen create large stores of supplies?

Robert DePugh: Well some groups did.

Eric Beckemeier: Were there weapons and explosives included in those?

Robert DePugh: There was an article in one of the New York newspapers (inaudible).

Eric Beckemeier: I know I've looked up a lot of the, on the computer you can look up the old *New York Times* articles, I have found quite a few about the Minutemen activities in New York but I don't know if I've seen the article you're talking about or not. It's been a long time.

Robert DePugh: I think they said tons, you know, tons of guns and ammunition and so forth, and so I imagine they had a good supply and there were others but that was always on the state level.

Eric Beckemeier: So to the best of your knowledge did the FBI set up surveillance on you or any of the other members?

Robert DePugh: Always. Always and I'm not sure it ever stopped. I would guess they probably have a copy of every e-mail I've ever sent and every e-mail I've ever received right up to today. They've got nothing to do but spend money and once they find something to spend it on why quit?

Eric Beckemeier: Yeah. So can you tell me a little about your legal problems you know at the time from being involved in the Minutemen?

Robert DePugh: Well let me through and let me see if I can find. (Pause). So the Patriotic party and the American party existed at the same time but we did not have the coordination, you know. That was where the individualists were at a loss because we were not doing what we didn't know about each other and so there was no national third party ever made to form.

Eric Beckemeier: Yeah.

Robert DePugh: I will begin to try to put some of this stuff together but that is just a sample of one of the, you're talking about my legal problems of which I had never ending legal problems, but I was arrested dozens and at least a dozen times.

Eric Beckemeier: So basically every time there was any possible reason for them to arrest you, you feel like that's what they did?

Robert DePugh: I was arrested, and of at least a dozen times I was indicted, I was only convicted twice. That means there was ten times at least that I was found not guilty. I was not convicted but of all those ten or twelve times I had to fight with the little bit of time, and little bit of help, and little bit of money that I had. I was fighting the whole federal bureaucracy and that would be just one little part that that you're holding [at this point the author is holding a case brief from one of DePugh's appeal cases]. That was just one little part of those ten cases, you know, most of the time I did my own legal work. You know I've been diagnosed with Amyotrophic Lateral Sclerosis, generally called Lou Gehrig's disease, so as I set here now my average lifespan is maybe a year and I have a lot I'd like to do in that year. But, you know, people talk about life expectancy usually think in terms of someone who has heart disease that, you know, will have a little time to feel generally well until they fall over dead but with ALS it's not that way. I'm in considerable pain right now. I'll be in considerable pain until the day I die so I'm not going to be able to do near what I would like to do but if I could do it all one of the many books I would write would be titled *Never Trust a Lawyer.* You know I was sold out time after time after time by my own attorney, you know. They would trade off. For example, in one case the federal prosecutor, he had a case going at the same time he was prosecuting me. The defendants in that case were a bunch of young people who were mostly men who were all sons of some of the old time mafia hoods who had been all indicted on narcotics cases. My lawyer was defending those same people at the same time he was defending me. (Off the record) (Pause) That's one of the times I was convicted but most of the time I had to do it myself.

Eric Beckemeier: So the first time you were convicted, is that when you wrote *Beyond the Iron Mask*? Or was that awaiting appeal?

Robert DePugh: I wrote *Beyond the Iron Mask* before I was convicted the first time and of course, you know, from my point of view the government prosecutors had absolutely no conscience. For example, my last arrest came after they searched my house there in Norborne, my wife's house which was in her name, and supposedly for child pornography. I forget just what the term is they use for that but it was a pretextual search, you know. They got the search warrant for one thing in order to search for something else. The guns I was convicted of possessing were not mine. After my first arrest and the seizure of these guns I made another stupid mistake. Under the laws in the state of Missouri a wife owns half of everything the husband owns. I filed a motion to get my guns back. I said you have seized property that belongs to my wife. So my brother Bill received a call from the BATF that, well, "What do want us to do with these guns that belong to Bob's wife?" So he took the pickup truck and went down and got the guns and for a while they were stored at Biolab and I said to Van. I said "Well let's get one thing straight. They're your guns," you know. And eventually a lot of them ended up in Van's front closet and in the basement so when they searched her house, supposedly for the child pornography, there were these guns and that is really the thing that broke my family up, you know, was the. All my wife had to do was say "Yep, they're mine," but she wouldn't do that. She found it easier to sue for divorce after eleven years.

Eric Beckemeier: What year was it that you were arrested for that the second time?

Robert DePugh: Well I would have to look it up to find out for sure but I think, let's see, I'm eighty-four and that happened when I was sixty-nine.

Eric Beckemeier: It would've been like '91. So is that when you finally moved away from Norborne for good was after that?

Robert DePugh: That's about the time that my wife. After she got divorced she may have continued to live in that house for a few years. I'm not sure.

Eric Beckemeier: So altogether how much time did you spend in prison for these convictions?

Robert DePugh: About seven years, four and a half and two and a half.

Eric Beckemeier: So did you ever officially step down as leader of the Minutemen?

Robert DePugh: Well there was no proclamation.

Eric Beckemeier: So when did the Minutemen kind of start to decline? I mean there's still some operating even today but when did they kind of start declining?

Robert DePugh: Well with my first arrest, you know, we'll say. That was the devastating blow for us. At about the same time some of the other groups were arrested in New York and California. At the national level and at the state level it fell apart once the only active organizations left were the band level, you know, which was (inaudible).

Eric Beckemeier: Yeah. Umm could you tell me a little about the Committee of Ten Million?

Robert DePugh: Well basically that was set up in '67.

Eric Beckemeier: Were they kind of did they work with the Minutemen or was it separate from?

Robert DePugh: We formed another organization that was called the Inter-organizational Coordinating Committee. We had our first meeting in Norborne. Then we had two or three national meetings. Both of the two main ones were held in Kansas City. That was an attempt to bring together all of these various organizations that operated separately into one group that would be able to operate collectively but once again individualism out won collectivism. We never worked together.

Eric Beckemeier: Was the *American Nationalist* a publication of one of these organizations that you were talking about?

Robert DePugh: What?

Eric Beckemeier: The *American Nationalist*. I found it online, I was looking for resources and your name was mentioned with the Committee of Ten Million and the

American Nationalist being like a publication. Kind of like a newsletter almost.

Robert DePugh: Never heard of it.

Eric Beckemeier: Huh. Interesting what you'll find on the computer sometimes.

Robert DePugh: Yeah.

Eric Beckemeier: Yeah. Are the Minutemen in the American Southwest who claim to be protecting the border related in any way to your Minutemen?

Robert DePugh: Well yes and no. Some of those people are former members and they wrote to me for like a quote endorsement and I told them "Do your thing, leave me out of it."

Eric Beckemeier: So do you think they got their name from you all or did they?

Robert DePugh: Who knows?

Eric Beckemeier: Also, you published a pamphlet *What's Wrong with Communism?* Do you remember what year that was? I got a copy and it doesn't have a year on it. I'm kind of curious just for reference?

Robert DePugh: I don't know.

Eric Beckemeier: How often and for how long was *On Target* published?

Robert DePugh: Did I give you a copy?

Eric Beckemeier: You did give me a copy.

Robert DePugh: Well I'll have to say it will be in round numbers, you know. From 1955 to, well, I'm gonna say 1980 because I don't really remember if that was the last issue or not.

Eric Beckemeier: Well that's what I just needed because I hadn't been able to find that. Was it monthly, most of the time anyway?

Robert DePugh: Yeah.

Eric Beckemeier: And just a little bit, could you just tell me a little bit about Biolab, I know we talked about it earlier, but what type pharmaceuticals did you manufacture?

Robert DePugh: Well we made both but it was eighty percent veterinary.

Eric Beckemeier: And, uh, this is kind of off the subject but at one time I guess you had a building in Independence, and I guess there was an explosion that damaged that building.

Robert DePugh: Well I guess there was one time an explosion if you can call it that.

Eric Beckemeier: Do you think that was an attack on you or the Minutemen, or was it just random, or did one of your own members maybe do it?

Robert DePugh: I really don't know. I don't think it was random but I don't know. I think it was sort of a psychological warfare type of thing to scare us because we did the same thing to them. So I couldn't say if it was a disgruntled right-winger that did it, we had those too.

Eric Beckemeier: As far as for all of members that were arrested in New York for the plotting to bomb the Communist camps was that something that you had any knowledge of, or was there even a plan to do the bombings?

Robert DePugh: As I heard it, you know, sort of after the fact. Well I may be thinking of two different things here now. The group in Connecticut had decided that they were going to burn down this what they thought was a Communist training camp and they were uh informed on by one of the members in the Connecticut group.

Eric Beckemeier: Uh huh.

Robert DePugh: So I think it was the Connecticut State Police that ambushed these Minutemen from Connecticut and shot one of them. I remember he was, the bullet almost killed him, went in one eye and cut out the other eye so he was blind totally. I don't remember exactly how all that happened. Some of the people were obviously arrested. I don't remember now how all that turned out.

Eric Beckemeier: Well I think that's about all I have for now but do you think in the future sometime you would be willing to interview again?

Robert DePugh: Well what I would suggest is that I will get a box and start putting stuff in it and the next time you stop by I might have it all ready for ya.

Eric Beckemeier: OK. Anything at all will be helpful to me.

Robert DePugh: OK.

Acknowledgments

The goal of this book was to provide an accurate historical record of Robert DePugh's Minutemen. Due to the amount of time that has elapsed since the downfall of the Minutemen this was an arduous task that I could not have accomplished without much help and support.

A very special thanks is due to Bob DePugh. He has always been available to answer questions concerning the Minutemen and perhaps most importantly he was willing to share information in the interview included in the appendix of this book that could not have been obtained anywhere else. Bob DePugh is truly one of the last available sources of much of the information concerning the Minutemen and his cooperation is greatly appreciated.

A special thanks is also due to Dr. Dane C. Miller, professor of Criminal Justice, who was my mentor in this work when it was my Honors Project at the University of Central Missouri. He was a great help in suggesting corrections and reading through this project. Without him the quality of this work would be significantly less than it is today.

I also want to thank the Honors College staff and administration at the University of Central Missouri for giving me the opportunity to write a more lengthy work than I had ever attempted before. Without the Honors Project there would be no book.

Finally, I want to thank my family and friends for their patience with me while I spent long hours writing this book and more recently while I was preparing it for publication. Without my family's support I may have never had the courage and determination to finish this project.